A Christian Book of the Dead

Accompanying their journey after death

Margarete van den Brink
and Hans Stolp

Hawthorn Press

A Christian Book of the Dead © 2004 Margarete van den Brink and Hans Stolp

Margarete van den Brink and Hans Stolp are hereby identified as authors of this work in accordance with Section 77 of the Copyright, Designs and Patent Act, 1988. They assert and give notice of their moral right under this Act.

Published by Hawthorn Press, Hawthorn House, 1 Lansdown Lane, Stroud, Gloucestershire, GL5 1BJ, UK
Tel: (01453) 757040 Fax: (01453) 751138
info@hawthornpress.com
www.hawthornpress.com

Cover image St. Matthew and The Angel, 1655-60 (oil on canvas) by Rembrandt Harmensz. van Rijn (1606-69). Louvre, Paris, France/Bridgeman Art Library
Cover design by Patrick Roe at Southgate Solutions
Typeset at Hawthorn Press by Lynda Smith
Printed in the UK by The Cromwell Press, Trowbridge, Wiltshire
Printed on acid-free paper from managed forests

First published in the Netherlands by Uitgeverij Ankh-Hermes under the title
Omgaan met Gestorvenen
This edition © Hawthorn Press 2004
Translated by Tony Langham

British Library Cataloguing in Publication Data applied for

ISBN 1 903458 31 5

Contents

?

Foreword

Having had the privilege of working with other people on the theme of life beyond life, I came to realise that many people around us have experiences connected with the so-called dead. However, in the prevailing age of materialism, they are diffident about sharing their experiences, understandably so.

Nevertheless, in moments of deep conversation they might find the courage to do so. Then, I believe, you would gradually find that among your acquaintances a whole series of phenomena surrounding the death experience would come to light.

Do you remember, as a child, having books in which numbered dots were spread over a blank page? By joining these apparently disconnected dots together a picture 'suddenly' appears. I am convinced that if you make such an experiment you would be amazed at the intimations already present in society, but which remain disconnected. It is as though we have to find our brothers and sisters, meet them on a deeper than normal level for these markers to be shared; simple, profound, meaningful experiences, which give startling insights that we are more than our physical bodies and have rudimentary faculties which exceed those of the five senses.

To encourage you to make your own search I will briefly outline a few examples in my own experience. On one occasion I was woken up at about 1.30 am by my wife: 'I have just had a frightening dream – something terrible has happened to Joan'. Joan was a friend of ours, and it turned out that at the very time of the dream she had been killed in a motorcar accident. These rudimentary intimations that we can reach out to others beyond the limit of the five senses have been secretly developed by the USA and Russian intelligence services for espionage purposes; selected sensitive people have been trained to practise so-called remote viewing techniques (see 'Psychic Warrior' by David Morehouse).

My mother-in-law – 'Grandma' – lived in a home for the elderly. My son, who lived some distance away, decided to take her out for coffee and called in to see us before he went to pick her up. An hour earlier, we had had a telephone call to tell us that Auntie Margery had died at 3:00 am that morning. She was a close friend of Grandma's. We suggested to our son that he break the news gently after they had had their coffee. In the restaurant Grandma said: 'Do you know, I had such a strange experience last night. I was woken up by someone, at about 3:00 am, who came into my room and stood at the bottom of my bed and after a while said goodbye and went out. I rang the bell for matron, who insisted no one had come in to visit. I don't understand it!' 'I think I can explain it, Grandma,' said my son. 'You see Margery died last night and came to say goodbye.'

Grandma was like that; she had many interesting, so-called waking dreams. For instance, in one of her dreams she saw her husband, who had died some fifty or more years earlier, on the other side of a river. 'Can I cross over now?' she called. 'Not yet, Edna,' came the reply, 'but I will be here when you do.' 'Funny,' she said ... 'the river was called Sticks'. 'How do you spell it?' I asked. 'Sticks I suppose.' I then spoke of the Greek description of the river crossed by the soul at death – the river Styx. 'Well I never!' she responded.

In this book you will find many examples of such experiences, and in far more detail, that can illuminate the whole field of growing insight into the life after death and the relation of souls in the spiritual world to those of us still on earth. We have to overcome the prevailing, impoverished image of the human being and wake up to what our own inner experience tells us:

Firstly, I am more than my body.

Secondly, I can gain some slender knowledge of the invisible realities in which I live: my thoughts, feeling impulses – my relationships – all so vital, that give my life a sense of meaning or reality.

Winston Churchill has described man as 'a spiritual creature advancing on an immortal destiny, and science, politics and economics are good or bad inasmuch as they help or hinder him on his eternal journey'. Don't just use this book for information but as an encouragement to take a new step on your journey into the sphere of the spirit – the soul's true home. Your friends who are already there will help you.

Russell Evans, author of *Helping Children to Overcome Fear*

Introduction

What happens to us when we die? Many people believe that life after death is a reality. Many more simply do not know. For large numbers of people the idea of life after death is wishful thinking.

But is death really the country from which 'no traveller returns'?

This age-old question which faces us all, whether we ourselves are close to death or have to deal with the death of a loved one, inspired us to write this book.

Sometimes living with the question is as much as we can do: any easy answer may only be the closing of a door in ourselves. In this book, drawing on actual near-death experiences and people's real experience of keeping alive their relationship with those who have died, we try to open doors and suggest possibilities that are not just wishful thinking or fixed certainties.

It is easy to leap to easy, hasty conclusions. It seems that the scientific age, which has also exerted a powerful influence on Christianity, often too hastily dismisses what it does not fathom. But in doing so perhaps it shuts the door on whole realms of experience that cannot be quantified or measured in material terms.

In our time more and more people have the inner certainty that death is not the end. But if it is not the end, what then happens beyond death?

The answers to this question can be found in eastern religions, but surprisingly also in the Christian tradition! In fact they were prevalent in Christianity originally, but got lost in mainstream Christianity. They were, however, passed on in secret for centuries and still exist.

In this book we wish to focus attention once again on the views contained in this hidden Christianity.

These views clearly reveal what happens when someone dies, and how this path then continues through the spirit worlds. Their answer lies along the same lines as the answers provided to this question by eastern traditions.

We, the writers of this book, enjoyed working on it. We felt that we were not only fulfilling our own inner desires, but also letting quiet voices in the spiritual world speak and be heard.

This world calls upon us to put aside our fear of death and rediscover an inner trust in the ancient secrets of death and therefore also in the secrets of life itself. Anyone who can put aside his fear of death will also put aside the fear of life and will be able to face life here and now in an open-minded way. Therefore the insights in this book can help not only to change customary ideas about death and our feeling about it, but also our attitude to life.

Many of us who have lost loved ones continue an inner life and conversation with them. Perhaps we light a candle beside their photograph, or in some way celebrate their birthday or the day they died. In this way, we intuitively and spontaneously express the ancient knowledge that true love is eternal and never comes to an end. What we often do not do is reflect on the fact that our loved one on the other side also remains involved with us and continues to surround us with love.

Backed up by the countless stories of others who have had similar experiences, we the authors became convinced that we remain connected with those who have died. In this book we want to show how the living and the dead can relate to each other in this new situation. What can we on earth do for our loved ones in the spiritual world? And what does our loved one in the spiritual world do for us? Insights in this matter help us to relate to each other in a new way, certainly just as intensely as in the past.

Before you start to read this book we would like to express a wish. Try not only to understand the contents with your head, but also with your heart. By doing so you will discover that ancient wisdom about life and life after death is no longer something new and strange to you but expresses a deeper truth. This deeper truth – which lives hidden in the souls and hearts of all of us – reveals itself to us when we create the inner atmosphere to hear it.

Margarete van den Brink and Hans Stolp

1. The Tragedy of Traditional Christianity

All the major religions and spiritual movements are based on the idea of life after death. Ancient documents, such as the *Brihadaranyaka Upanishad*, *The Egyptian Book of the Dead*, and *The Tibetan Book of the Dead*, contain vivid descriptions of the path which a person who has died takes in the 'afterlife'. The Bible also writes about this, both in the Old and New Testaments. Life after death has always been acknowledged in Christianity.

When the scientific age dawned, and with it the age of technology and a sense of the material world as ultimate reality, it became increasingly difficult to see beyond the 'veil' of the senses to other forms of existence that had been self-evident to the great religions. The content of religion came to be ascribed to 'mere imagination': we had finally grown up and arrived at the quantifiable truth – and it was a hard one: this life is all there is, and our minds, bodies, hearts and wills just a random – though admirable – congregation of atoms and electrical impulses.

But while doubts about life after death have continued to grow in society, there is – rather curiously – an increasing interest in everything related to death, dying and life after death. Lectures and workshops on the subject of life after death attract hundreds of people. In addition, there are endless books on this subject. People's questions are also becoming more specific and increasingly penetrating. In many cases they are the result of extraordinary personal experiences, for example the loss of a loved one or a near-death experience. It is as though we have a sense that there is still a great deal to be said on the subject of life after death and want to know more about it. But where can we go with all these questions? The traditional Christian Church can no longer help much here. There is every possible shade of Christian belief, from pragmatic humanism to literal belief in the virgin birth and the Resurrection, but the Church itself is of course subtly influenced by modern consciousness; and anyway, surely, we are no longer satisfied by knowledge imparted from on high: we want to know things for ourselves.

Some time ago there was an interview with a Church minister from The Hague, Carel ter Linden, in the *Trouw* newspaper, on the occasion of the publication of his book, 'A country where you don't know the way'.[2] It is about people who are mourning the death of a loved one. Ter Linden collected the material for his book over fifteen years while observing groups who were mourning their loved ones. As he was finishing his book, he found that his own wife was terminally ill. She died a year later. When the interviewer asked Ter Linden how he saw life after death himself, he answered:

> That is the most difficult question you could ask me. At best we can hope for something, suspect something, trust in something. I hope that I will 'see' God at last. That some of the secrets of this world and this life will be revealed. I would so much like to look behind the screens just once. At the same time, reason tells me that this is impossible. People used to think that they had an immortal soul which broke away from the mortal body and returned to God. For many believers this is no longer an acceptable idea. Our soul lives because our brain lives, but when it dies, our soul will also die.

Nevertheless, and almost against my own better judgement, I continue to hope that my faith will enable me to behold something, if only for a moment.

However, perhaps living on with God does not mean that we will 'behold Him', so much as that we will 'live on in people'. Whatever has been said and done in God's spirit is not lost, but survives as a small link in God's history.[3]

These words show a person who has a deep desire for God in his heart and hopes that he will learn the truth about God's existence after death. At the same time, his reason tells him that this desire is impossible and unreal. After all, science has taught us that what we call the soul can only live because we have a brain. When we die, our body dies and therefore our brain dies, as well as our soul. In other words, nothing is left of us.

Ter Linden's words clearly show that he, and therefore his Church, no longer knows the most important answers to questions about our human existence. Yet people have a great desire for real answers. This applies particularly to those who have had profound religious experiences themselves: for example out of body experiences, near-death experiences, travelling in the spiritual world or in heaven, encounters with loved ones who have died and so on: experiences for which there is still no room in the traditional churches.

However, as people of our time, we want to understand these matters and these events so that we can place them in a context, both in our own lives and in a wider context. Let us see if actual experience can begin to unearth them.

Notes

1   Morehouse, David: *Psychic Warrior*, Clairview Books, US 2000
2   Carel ter Linden: *Een land waar je de weg niet kent*
3   *Trouw*, 10 March 1997.

2. The Lost Secret

I'll never forget the first time I had one of those experiences. I'd gone to bed, read my book for a while, and finally put it away and turned off the light to go to sleep. Suddenly and quite unexpectedly, I was hanging just below the ceiling and looking down on my body, which was lying quietly on the bed, without moving. I remember immediately thinking rather feverishly: How can this happen and what does it mean? Although I had turned off the light, I could still clearly see my body lying on the bed. In addition, I could feel that I still had a 'body', arms and legs, but that this body was transparent. I could hardly see it myself, but I could feel it.

When I realised this, I started to think about everything I had learned during my theological studies. I had been taught that people used to believe we have a body and a soul, but that this idea was out of date. After all, the body and the soul were one, and could not be separated from each other. As I had understood it, it was better to forget about the idea of a soul. But while I was hanging up close to the ceiling, it seemed to me that this old distinction was not so crazy after all. At that moment I was actually separated from my body. I could look down on it as an object, and at the same time I could continue to think and move, and I had feelings and emotions. Therefore I could, it seemed, exist separately from my body.

This, and subsequent experiences, inspired me to look for an answer. What exactly are we, what are we composed of, how do we work? Incidentally, many people have out of body experiences like mine these days. There is nothing special about it. And many people seek a new direction in life as a result. They want to understand what has happened to them, in order to be able to place it in context in their lives.

As I sought to understand my own experience and those of others, I came across St. Paul, the great Apostle of Christianity. St. Paul said that man consisted of a body, a soul and a spirit:

And the very God of peace sanctify you wholly, and I pray God your whole spirit and soul and body be preserved blameless into the coming of Our Lord Jesus Christ.[1]

Therefore St. Paul sees man as consisting of three distinct elements, two of which are non-material. St. Paul himself regularly had these out of body experiences during his lifetime. When this happened he went 'up to the third heaven', that is to say, he had an experience of rising up to the highest world of light. In the following quotation, St. Paul speaks in the third person as though he is talking about someone else, but it is generally assumed that this was for reasons of modesty. He wrote:

I knew a man in Christ, fourteen years ago ... such as one caught up to the third heaven. And I knew such a man ... how he was taken up into paradise, and heard unspeakable words, which it is not lawful for a man to utter.[2]

When St. Paul says that he was 'caught up to the third heaven', this means that during his out-of-the-body experience, his journey to heaven, he was able to rise up to the highest world of light. He was initiated there into the great cosmic secrets which are 'not lawful for a man to utter', and which cannot be expressed in our simple three-dimensional human language. Other people have made similar journeys to heaven.

Apart from the fact that St. Paul travelled to heaven in an out of body experience (we can assume that it was not just once), he was also an initiate: on one occasion, which lasted three days, he was initiated by angels into spiritual secrets which are hidden to us people on earth. This is shown in the famous story about St. Paul being suddenly surrounded by radiant heavenly light when he was on his way to Damascus to persecute the Christians there. He heard Jesus Christ himself talking to him from that light, (the Master who had died and risen again according to his disciples). In this story it is said of St. Paul that subsequently

'...he was three days without sight, and neither did he eat or drink ...'[3]

If someone does not drink for three days in the Middle East, something is definitely wrong. In the hot climate there, drinking is essential for life. Added to this, it is said that St. Paul was blind for three days. We now start to realise what had actually happened. St. Paul had entered a spiritual world while his body was lying in his bed in a coma, apparently dead. This spiritual journey lasting three and a half days was quite a special experience in those ancient times, but not all that unusual for the different consciousness of those days. During this initiation he travelled in his spiritual body far into the spiritual world, acquiring the kinds of knowledge and insight which cannot be found here on earth when we are bound to our physical body. Incidentally, this sort of initiation is described in other places in the Bible, for example in the story of the prophet Jonah, who spent three days in the belly of a whale.

The knowledge which St. Paul wrote about in his letters in

the Bible is therefore knowledge which he acquired when he was initiated during his travels in heaven. When he describes the true nature of man he does this on the basis of these insights. In the ancient esoteric or spiritual tradition of Christianity, St. Paul's description of man as being three in one (i.e., consisting of three parts or elements) is developed into a 'four in one'. However, this 'four in one' is actually no more than a more detailed version of St. Paul's original description.

What is St. Paul actually saying, and what does he mean when he says a person consists of a body, a soul and a spirit?

What St. Paul simply calls the 'body' is divided in the esoteric tradition into the 'physical body' and the 'ethereal body'.[4] After all, our body lives because of the divine cosmic energy which constantly flows through it, giving it life. If this cosmic energy were to cease for even one moment, our body would fall down dead. This cosmic energy, or the ethereal body, is sometimes referred to as 'prana' in Eastern traditions. In the Bible, reference is sometimes made to 'the breath of God'. For example, in Genesis the creation of Adam is described as follows:

And the Lord God formed man of the dust of the ground, and breathed into his nostrils the breath of life; and man became a living soul.[5]

It could hardly be said more clearly: God creates the physical body of man and then brings it to life by surrounding it and permeating it with cosmic energy, the 'breath of life'. This ethereal body flows all through our physical body and slightly extends beyond our physical body. It is therefore actually like a second transparent body (only visible to those with clairvoyant perception).

What St. Paul calls our 'soul' is known as the 'astral body' in the esoteric tradition. This word 'astral' comes from the Latin word 'astrum' (plural: astra) which means star or constellation.

This reveals that our soul or our astral body is the bearer of our 'astral forces': the different forces which we are given by the various planets and which determine our character in this incarnation. In a sense, we could say that our soul or our astral body represents the drives and emotions of our ego, in which we experience ourselves. We could also say: our astral body is the bearer of our self or of the forces of the self. This astral body also permeates our physical body and extends far beyond our physical body. (These days, the ethereal and astral body together are sometimes referred to as our aura.) Thus the astral body forms a third, invisible body.

What St. Paul called our 'spirit' is sometimes referred to as our 'higher Self' in the esoteric tradition. We can also say that this refers to the divine spark which slumbers in each of us. This 'spirit' or 'Self' therefore has three bodies in our life on earth: the first is the astral body. The second is the ethereal body. And the third is our physical body. These three bodies ensure that our real Self (or our spirit or our true spiritual essence, our divine core) is almost invisible and concealed behind all these bodies. This almost hidden divine core is eternal in us and cannot die.

Undoubtedly, St. Paul was aware of this division of man into four elements. However, these insights were part of the secret mystery knowledge which was never spoken about in public in those ancient times, but only in the privacy of disciples' circles.

It was not only St. Paul who followed this system of public and secret doctrines in those ancient times; every Master did so in the past, including Jesus himself, Buddha and many others. Why did they do this? They did so because it was the custom in all the initiation- and mystery-schools. These schools existed in every country in pre-Christian times. There were famous ones, for example in Heliopolis in Egypt, in Eleusis and Delphi in Greece, at the school of Pythagoras in Italy, and also in Persia, India and other places in the world. Everyone who visited these schools had to promise to keep the knowledge which they learnt there completely secret. Breaking this rule was punished by death. This secrecy was so important because the knowledge which was acquired through initiation could, on the one hand, only be understood by those who had followed a certain esoteric training.

On the other hand, it contained fundamental knowledge about cosmic energy. This insight can be compared to knowledge about nuclear energy. It therefore could not simply be passed on to all and sundry. For what would happen if it fell into the hands of someone obsessed with power?

St. Paul, Jesus, Buddha and many others participated in this tradition of initiation and therefore visited mystery schools. In that way they learned to distinguish between general knowledge and secret knowledge. That is why when St. Paul talked about the nature of the human being in public, he only referred in a simplified form to man as 'three in one' and did so without any further explanation. An explanation would have meant that he would have to reveal secret knowledge, which he neither wanted nor was able to do.

Once I had discovered the trail of these ancient insights I started to understand a little more about my own out of body experience. When I was hanging up there by the ceiling, separated from my body, I was not dead, for I was able to return to my body again afterwards. This was because my non-material soul and spiritual 'bodies' may have left my physical body, but they were still connected to it by a silver cord. This silver cord is also referred to in the Bible: death only occurs when the silver cord is untied or cut through. Without further explanation, the Bible states:

… or ever the silver cord be loosed …Then shall the dust return to the earth as it was: and the spirit shall return unto God who gave it.[6]

The fact that this is simply stated without any explanation clearly shows that this knowledge was part of the secret insights, only available to those 'with ears to hear': the initiates.

St. Paul and many Christians of the first centuries were still wholly familiar with this threefold nature of man; with the fact that human beings are not only part of the physical world through their physical bodies, but are also part of a non-physical world of soul and spirit. However, during the third and fourth centuries, spiritual or esoteric Christianity was increasingly branded as heresy by more orthodox, Church-oriented Christians and was prohibited and eradicated. The spiritual gnostic texts which contain much of this old secret knowledge were also forbidden and destroyed. From that time onwards, such knowledge was only passed on in secret, for example by the followers of Mani, the Waldenses and Cathars. For centuries no one knew anything about this spiritual tradition and secret knowledge except for those who belonged to such traditions. In 1945, ancient gnostic texts were rediscovered in Nag Hammadi in Egypt. They finally brought a secret knowledge back to light, as did modern esoteric traditions, such as theosophy and Rudolf Steiner's anthroposophy.

With the loss of these spiritual gnostic texts in the third and fourth centuries, ancient insight into the nature of the human being also gradually disappeared, so in subsequent centuries people no longer understood what St. Paul had meant when he said that man consisted of a body, a soul and a spirit.

That is why the Council of Constantinople in 869 AD declared that man only has a body and a soul, not a spirit. In that year, man's true divine core, the spirit (or the higher, non-material self) was, one can say, abolished. The decision of this council reveals that in the ninth century no one any longer had insight into the secret knowledge which St. Paul once attained and which was expressed in his description of man as threefold being. The decision of that council was therefore a complete break with St. Paul's teachings.

At the same time this represented a darkening of vision of what occurs beyond death, when the silver cord is 'loosed' and the physical body decays. Prior to this time, people still had a sense that at death we enter the spiritual world as a spiritual being, clothed in an astral and an ethereal body, to start a new life there, a life at the spiritual level. This process by which man lost all understanding of what death is and what happens to people when they pass through the gates of death had already started, then, in 869 AD.

Thus while man lost his 'spirit' in the ninth century, at a later stage he also lost his soul. In the nineteenth century it was the philosopher Nietzsche who said that the soul is actually a negligible part of the human being:

The body is full of passions, let us leave the soul out of it.

He also wrote:

The soul is just a word for a trivial aspect of the body.[7]

These quotations from Nietzsche's work reveal that he sees the soul as a physical, and therefore mortal element. Basically, he sees man as a purely physical body. Through the centuries we can trace a development in which the human being is increasingly reduced to this physical body alone. He was first denied 'spirit' in the ninth century, and then denied 'soul' in the nineteenth and twentieth centuries.

In the nineteenth century, Nietzsche was merely expressing what more and more people thought and how they viewed the human being. This view, in which man is no more than a physical body, even became widespread in the churches. In the 1970s, Krop, a minister from Groningen, preaching to students on the radio and on television, voiced what many people in the church already thought. What he said more or less amounted to the fact that 'dead means dead', and we should stop trying to keep each other happy with stories about heaven (and hell). There simply is no life after death he said.

This is the logical consequence of reducing man to a purely physical body, of a view that, instructed and informed by modern science, recognises only what is physically tangible. Krop's view reflects the view of minister Ter Linden, who was referred to in the previous chapter.

The disappearance of the secret knowledge of man's true nature, a secret which was familiar to St. Paul and the spiritual Christians of the first centuries, has ultimately led to this total impotence of the churches of our time to provide any meaningful answers to questions about life and life after death.

This development is very tragic. It is this loss which led us to refer in the previous chapter to the 'Tragedy of Traditional Christianity.'

Notes

1. I Thessalonians 5:23
2. 2 Corinthians 12:2-4.
3. Acts 9:9
4. For the different bodies constituting the human being we have given the names used by Rudolf Steiner. Other, different names are possible too. Rudolf Steiner's terminology, however, corresponds most closely to the little that is said about them in biblical texts. A more detailed description of these different bodies can be found in Steiner's book *Theosophy*.
5. Genesis 2:7
6. Judges 12:6, 7
7. Quoted from Nietzsche in: *Rittelmeyer: Gemeinschaft mit den Verstorbenen*, 1978

3. *Opening Up the Spiritual World*

These days, more and more people are having what they sense to be 'spiritual' experiences. Some of these are spontaneous out of body experiences as described in the previous chapter, while other people have had experiences of travelling in the spiritual world or in the heavenly world, sometimes as a consequence of a near-death experience. Many such experiences are closely linked with death and dying.

Descriptions of three personal experiences follow below: a near-death experience, a journey through the spiritual world as a result of a near-death experience, and finally a journey through the heavenly world which occurred spontaneously.

A near-death experience

Bo Katzmann lives in Switzerland and is the conductor of a successful choir. In an interview in a Swiss newspaper he describes a serious car accident he was involved in when he was twenty-one years old. He was admitted to hospital and had an operation. During this operation he had a near-death experience. In the interview he described this as follows:

> During the operation, after the accident, I heard the doctor saying: 'His heart has stopped beating. Give me the

resuscitation machine straightaway!' At the same time, I realised that I was floating up by the ceiling of the room and that my body was lying on the operating table. I could hear the thoughts of everyone who was present as though they were talking out loud. I floated down, and wanted to take the doctor's arm to point out that he could stop because I was dead. To my surprise, my arm went right through his body and he did not hear me at all.

Did he feel frightened or constricted in any way? Katzmann said:

Not at all. I felt completely peaceful, and all that excitement about my lifeless body seemed unnecessary. It was an indescribable feeling not to be imprisoned in that narrow constrictive body any more. Attracted by a force, I floated out of the room and found myself in a sort of world space surrounded by mists. All knowledge was present in this 'mist' and as a spiritual being, I was part of this 'all-encompassing knowledge'. The answers to all the questions that exist were to be found there. Perceiving so much knowledge all at once was like an inner explosion. But all this was nothing compared to the light I saw.

The interviewer asked: 'What sort of light was it?'

Actually, it was only light in the second instance, in the first instance it was love. Love which was so strong that it simply radiated everywhere, a very personal love which surrounded me and attracted me to it. I could not see the source of the light, only an indication of it, and even that was hardly bearable.

The interviewer asked: 'The doctors brought you back to life. What was that like for you?' Katzmann replied:

As I was being pulled towards the light, something was stopping me and I knew that I had to go back, that there was something waiting for me, a task I still had to fulfil. For three weeks I was in the intensive care department connected to a ventilator and a life-support machine which fed me. After four months I was able to leave the hospital, and life seemed very hard. It took me a long time to regain my will and strength for life. However, in retrospect, I see everything that happened as a merciful event.

When he was asked whether he now thinks differently about life and death, he answered:

'I certainly do. I now enjoy life again. I have seen that death is like a birth and that true life only starts after our life on earth.'[1]

Looking further into the spiritual world

George Ritchie also had a near-death experience. He describes this in his book, *Return from Tomorrow*. Shortly after 'dying' as the result of serious lung disease, he encountered a radiant figure of light, whom he called Jesus, in his hospital room. Surrounded by this light and love, he first looked back over his past life. The special aspect of this experience is that Jesus took him along and showed him different areas in the spiritual world. He exhorted Ritchie to keep his eyes upon Him. They then went on an extraordinary journey. Ritchie wrote:

It wasn't like the out of body travel I'd experienced earlier. Then, my own thoughts had obsessed me. Then I'd seemed almost to skim the surface of the earth. Now we were higher, moving faster; and with my eyes on Him, as he commanded, this mode of movement no longer seemed strange or alarming.

To begin with, they visited a number of towns on earth, both large and small towns. Ritchie saw factories, busy streets, houses and people walking around, working, drinking and smoking. To his surprise, he saw other people walking and moving about amongst these people, asking them something or wanting to tell them something, but without being heard or perceived by them. In fact, they were not seen at all. Ritchie suddenly realised that these people were dead, just as he was. Some of them tried to get hold of cigarettes or a drink, but were unable to do so because their hands went straight through everything. Others walked after the living and tried to say something to them. For example, he heard them giving advice about business transactions, exhortations to look after their health better, as well as regrets about the sorrow they had caused. It gradually became clear to him that the world where the people who have died exist is not far away from earth but is contained within it, within everyday life.

He was shown even more. He saw that there are people who have died, but who continue to hold onto the material world with their desires. He also saw people who had died, but are imprisoned in their own emotions and thought patterns, in their own hatred or destructive or perverse thoughts.

Ritchie came to the conclusion that death is completely different from the picture he previously had of it. Gradually he noticed other things. In the middle of all these myriads of people – those still alive on earth and those who have died – there were also other beings. These were large, radiant beings, bending over the living and the dead, full of compassion, to console them and encourage them. Angels! Ritchie wrote:

In fact, now that I had become aware of these bright presences, I realized with bewilderment that I'd been seeing them all along, without even consciously registering the fact.

16

The cities and towns which they had visited were also full of angels. They had been there in the streets and factories, in houses and even in pubs. But there had been nobody who could see them.

The journey continued, to yet another region. This region opened up because Ritchie started to distinguish a new world through the previous world. In this new region which he visited with the figure of light, Jesus, he entered an atmosphere of profound thought and knowledge, a sort of 'spiritual university' where discoveries were made which were far beyond his comprehension. The people who were working there – he did not know whether they were men or women – appeared to be absorbed by a goal which was bigger and more important than themselves. There was a sense of excitement when great discoveries were made. Ritchie wrote:

> Whatever else these people might be, they appeared utterly and supremely self-forgetful – absorbed in some vast purpose beyond themselves.

The journey continued, leaving earth far behind. They were now in an immense void, a nothingness, and the whole of this extensive emptiness appeared to vibrate with a 'sort of nameless promise'. Then in the infinite distance he saw…a city:

> A glowing, seemingly endless city, bright enough to be seen over all the unimaginable distance between. The brightness seemed to shine from the very walls and streets of this place, and from beings which I could now discern moving about within it. In fact the city and everything in it seemed to be made of light, even as the Figure at my side was made of light.

Overawed, Ritchie asked himself how it was possible that every building and every inhabitant could be so radiant that they were visible over a distance of many light years. While he was asking himself this… 'two of the bright figures seemed to detach themselves from the city and started towards us, hurling themselves across that infinity with the speed of light.'

However, Jesus and he then withdrew. The distance to the city and the two radiant beings became greater and greater, and the vision blurred. Ritchie wrote:

> Even as I cried out with loss, I knew that my imperfect sight could not now sustain more than an instant's glimpse of this real, this ultimate heaven.

The creature of light had shown him everything and explained everything he was ready for. Then he was enclosed by walls again and returned to his room in the hospital.

A voyage through the heavenly world

In his book 'The Holy Year'[2] Friedrich Rittelmeyer describes waking up one morning on Ascension Day and hearing a soft voice speaking to him. The voice asked: 'Would you like to see heaven?'

Behind him he saw an angel. Rittelmeyer wrote:

> He appeared to be bigger than me and made completely of light. It was as though he assimilated my whole being in himself. I can only describe the essence of this being as light and peace.

Rittelmeyer then describes in detail how there contact between him and the angel. When the angel spoke, Rittelmeyer at first only noticed that he wanted to say something, and that he, Rittelmeyer, needed to become very quiet inwardly to listen to him. He found that if the angel told you something, you would have to absorb this with your own being, not only with your thoughts, and help to create what he said in words yourself, with your inner self. It was only when your soul had become a quiet mirror that these words were clearly expressed, like the image of the sun on the smooth surface of a lake.

When the angel asked him whether he wanted to see heaven, Rittelmeyer surrendered himself with his whole being. He wrote:

> My soul slowly filled up with a fine spirituality. The spirit awakened in the world of the soul in a deeper and deeper sense. It was as though the space of the soul filled with invisible light which was full of love and life…

It seemed to him as though the light shone through the angel. It was only bearable because he constantly responded to it with an inner 'yes'. He felt that he had to ask questions, such as: 'Where are the people who have died?' As soon as he had spoken these words in the spirit he found himself in the world of the dead. He did not see anyone, but heard voices and a shifting, dynamic fullness of different sorts of human feeling. Once again he felt that he had to ask: 'Where is my mother?' – and there she was, very close as though she had been waiting for a long time. When Rittelmeyer focused on her being and listened, she said: 'I have been by your side more than you know. Why haven't you thought about me more? My warm love was a piece of heaven which was there for you.' He felt the warmth of the love with which she surrounded him. Apart from his mother, he also met other people he knew on earth who had died. He also asked to see people who had died and who were not yet present in the light.

Then he asked: 'Is this the world of the angels?' Worlds opened up, infinite throngs. It was only then that he understood why it is always said that angels sing. He discovered that they do not sing, but that their essence resounds:

Their soul incessantly sounds with gratitude to the Creator. So this is the eternal song of praise of the angels. It is the jubilation of more than a thousand voices, constantly changing and always present. Unheard by ears on earth, and yet filling all the heavens. Looking up at God's eternal works, they see immeasurable things which are still concealed from us people, while there are constantly new revelations opening up to them out of the divine world in their inner being.

What aspect of Christ can I see? When the word 'Christ' sounded, it was as though the whole of heaven sang. Everything shone and sparkled with joy for the acts which He performed on earth.

The joy about this became so tangible to Rittelmeyer that it was as though the angels were jubilant within him. Then he felt a healing force flowing from somewhere – from some hidden source. A healing force which was so strong and so pure that he felt his very body being cleansed. At the same time, he felt a divine goodness which filled him with heavenly bliss. It was such a divine force that he thought:

> People cannot understand or tolerate this yet. They will have to be educated with the words of Christ for centuries and millennia before this wonderful goodness can live in people. But then Christ will live in them too.

On his journey through the heavenly world, Rittelmeyer not only met beings who were well-disposed towards people, he also saw the spiritual opponents of Christ: the great Tempter and the Devil. He wrote:

> The great Tempter himself stood before me as a powerful figure …saying: 'I will give you all this if you fall down and worship

me.'…He really does speak like this when you see him. He spoke like this not only to Christ, but …already to Adam.

Then another realm arose from the depths, with a being full of omnipresent intellect. An intellect which contained all earthly thinking but which excluded heaven. The Devil? Yes, but very different from how we conceive him on earth. A prince, a ruler who is convinced that he already owns people. Rittelmeyer looked up at the angel and saw how he suffered. In his heart the name 'Christ' rose up. At the same moment that he thought this, the world crumpled all around him and disappeared. The name 'Christ' cannot be endured in these dark regions.

As he returned to his body, Rittelmeyer understood his task on earth. He sent a question up to heaven, 'Can I talk about my experiences?' The angel answered: 'What is given to one person is not given to him alone.' Then the doors to the heavenly worlds slowly closed again and Rittelmeyer was back on earth.

The consequences of these spiritual experiences

These are three experiences which people had 'on the other side'. They are very different in atmosphere, and yet they correspond closely. It is clear that for each of them, without a shadow of a doubt, there is a spiritual world or heaven. Nothing and no one will be able to dissuade them. This probably applies to anyone who has had such an experience.

A woman who had a near-death experience said:

Since that time my life has changed and been enriched. After the war I had become a humanist because of what I had heard about all the horrors of bombing and the extermination camps. I found it difficult to accept the existence of a God. But after this (near-death) experience, I do not just *believe* that there is a hereafter, *I am sure of it.* Even though it can never be proved that a near-death experience is the same as the experience of death, this is something I am certain of. I have really been able to look over the edge. It is an enormous feeling of enrichment that death is not the end.[3]

After this sort of experience, most people not only lose their fear of death, they have also undergone an inner change. Once they have been touched by the spiritual world, they feel like different, and better people. They are more interested in spiritual matters and have a greater interest in other people and in the beauty of creation. They also want to make a contribution themselves to a better world. Another woman talked about the change in her attitude to life after her near-death experience:

> But since I died, all of a sudden, right after my experience, I started wondering whether I had been doing the things I had done because they were good, or because they were good for *me.* Before, I just reacted off the impulse, and now I run things through my mind first, nice and slow. Everything seems to have to go through my mind and be digested first.
>
> I try to do things that have more meaning, and that makes my mind and soul feel better. And I try not to be biased, and not to judge people. I want to do things because they are good, not because they are good to me. And it seems the understanding I have of things now is so much better.[4]

When you ask people who have had these sorts of experiences whether they know themselves why they had these experiences or why they were shown worlds which are hidden for most people, they say that this was necessary to make people on earth aware of the fact that there is a spiritual world and that there is life after death.

Notes

1   Info-3 magazine, number 12, 1998, Info-3 Verlag (taken from *Anzeiger*, Breitenbach, Switzerland).
2   F. Rittelmeyer, *Das Heilige Jahr*, chapter 'Der Himmel'
3   P. van der Eijk, *Naar het hiernamaals en terug*
4   Raymond Moody: *Life After Life*

4. Looking Beyond the Boundary

When Jesus was baptised in the River Jordan at the age of thirty, the divine spirit, the spirit of Christ, descended upon Him and filled Him with enlightenment. Since that time He has been called Jesus Christ, because the divine spirit spoke through Him and in Him.

Five centuries earlier, Siddharta Gautama had found enlightenment sitting under a bodhi tree. From that moment he became known as the Buddha, the enlightened one. Both Buddha and Jesus Christ knew that this enlightenment could only be achieved by focusing your whole being on purity and love, leaving behind fear. They knew that this path to enlightenment was a path of purification, a path along which the divine spirit can come to light in us and start to speak through us, one in which our ego wholly serves this divine spirit.

When Jesus became enlightened He started upon a journey in which the divine spirit of Christ would increasingly fill him. Only when He died on the cross was this transformation complete: Jesus had become divine, wholly filled with the Christ: Jesus Christ. Man as God intended. In his footsteps we will follow. The spirit of Christ became man so that we human beings can develop the forces of Christ in us.

Both the Buddha and Jesus Christ, among many others, constantly speak about the path along which human beings must travel to reach the spirit. Life on earth is a journey, and *how* we travel this path is the important thing. What do we look for in this life? What do we want to achieve? The Buddha and Jesus Christ try to help us make the right choices, to guide us along a true path.

Jesus Christ, like the Buddha, was a man in whom all sorts of human potential developed which in us still lie deeply concealed as future potential. One of these capacities which developed fully in Jesus Christ was His ability to look directly into worlds of spirit. He was a 'seer' to an extent that we cannot even imagine.

This makes it more comprehensible that Jesus Christ could follow the path of people who had passed through death: He could follow them on the rest of their path through spiritual worlds. Only a few clairvoyants in our time have this kind of capacity, and to a far lesser extent.

However, it was very difficult for Jesus Christ to tell people what He could see in the spiritual world and about the journey of those who had died. People simply would not have understood that Jesus was able to speak so directly from his own observation. So when He wanted to talk about these things in public, Jesus chose to do so in the form of a story, which meant people could simply enter into the pictures He gave, taking them in with an open mind.

One of the stories which Jesus Christ tells about what He saw in the spiritual world concerns two people, a rich man and a poor man. They both die. In this story Jesus Christ describes what happens to them once they have crossed the river of death. The story is as follows:

There was a certain rich man, which was clothed in purple and fine linen, and fared sumptuously every day. And there was a certain beggar named Lazarus, which was laid at his gate, full of sores. And desiring to be fed with the crumbs which fell from the rich man's table; moreover, the dogs came and licked his sores. And it came to pass, that the beggar died, and was carried by the angels into Abraham's bosom; the rich man also died and was buried. And in hell he lifted up his eyes, being in torments, and seeth Abraham afar off, and Lazarus in his bosom.

And he cried and said, Father Abraham, have mercy on me, and send Lazarus, that he may dip the tip of his finger in water, and cool my tongue; for I am tormented in this flame.

But Abraham said, Son, remember that thou in thy lifetime receivedst thy good things, and likewise Lazarus evil things: but now he is comforted, and thou art tormented. And beside all this, between us and you there is a great gulf fixed: so that they which would pass from hence to you cannot; neither can they pass to us, that would come from thence.

Then he said, I pray thee therefore, father, that thou wouldest send him to my father's house: For I have five brethren; that he may testify unto them, lest they also come into this place of torment.

Abraham saith unto him, They have Moses and the prophets; let them hear them.

And he said, Nay, father Abraham: but if one went unto them from the dead, they will repent. And he said unto him, If they hear not Moses and the prophets, neither will they be persuaded, though one rose from the dead.[1]

This is a fascinating story. If we are able to listen through this story to what Jesus Christ is saying, we can find an incredible first-hand account of the 'other world', and about the life there that starts with our death.

The description of the life on earth of these two men is easy to recognise twenty centuries later. The rich man enjoys his possessions, his wealth, power and a luxurious and prosperous lifestyle. He *lives* for this. He has become addicted to eating and drinking and the 'good things' in life.

The poor man, Lazarus, is starving; he has scurvy and is covered in sores. Every day he lies by the entrance to the rich man's house, hoping that some scraps of the food piled up on the tables inside will fall from the table and be thrown to him. Every day he waits and hopes, usually in vain. The rich man must have seen poor Lazarus from time to time, right beside his front door, but every time he hurriedly walked by, holding his nose. It did not occur to him to use some of his wealth to change poor Lazarus' miserable destiny.

Lazarus learned the hard way that you cannot expect much help from people: they only care about themselves. It is precisely because of this that something else grew in him: a quiet surrender to God. When people don't help you, the only thing you can still hope for is help from God. A cry for help rises up in his heart. Sometimes, very occasionally, there is an answer to this cry, an answer in the form of a touch from the spiritual world. The nature of this answer can only be understood by those who have experienced this themselves, for such a touch evades any intellectual comprehension.

Both men, the rich man and the poor man die. Lazarus dies first. As soon as the silver cord was cut and he let go of his physical body, he saw a shining throng of light figures all around him, the angels who accompanied him to the spiritual world or heaven – described by Jesus Christ in these simple words: 'The beggar died, and was carried by the angels into Abraham's bosom.' This must have been an unimaginably joyous experience. For after all his suffering and all his loneliness, he was suddenly enveloped in an atmosphere of total peace and love.

What Lazarus experienced, suddenly seeing the angels in the hour of his death and being enveloped in this unimaginable peace radiated by them, is something which people can still experience today. You probably know – and perhaps have witnessed this yourself – that people sometimes start to 'shine' when they die: a glow of light can pass over their faces, which were drawn with pain and sorrow before.

When this happens, we get a sense that the dying person has, like Lazarus, been able to look beyond physical boundaries into a different realm. This experience is a sphere described as 'Abraham's bosom', an expression that indicates a state of true bliss. The eternal divine essence of Lazarus, his spirit or higher self, finds a safe haven in God's bosom, referred to here as Abraham's bosom. After all, for Jewish believers, Abraham evokes a range of feelings of surrender, trust, greatness and security in God.[2]

Therefore poor Lazarus did not struggle all his life in vain. In his desperate poverty and destitution, one thing remained: to trust in God with complete faith. It is this trust that made him aware and awakened this spirit in him.

The rich man had passed a very different life on earth. Because of his selfishness, sensuality and self-centredness the spirit in him could not reach the light. He did not learn to trust anyone or anything, nor to surrender himself. He did not focus on anyone or anything other than himself. He buried himself in his lower ego. This is why Jesus Christ describes the death of the rich man very differently from the death of poor Lazarus. He says: 'The rich man also died, and was buried. And in the realm of the dead he lifted up his eyes …'

When the rich man died he did not see any angels. Why not? Were the angels not there for him? They certainly were: everyone who dies is received, carried and accompanied by angels. But we only perceive them when we are able to see them and absorb their radiation. The rich man was actually unable to do this. During his lifetime he did not have any love, nor inner light, nor any attention for anyone other than himself. He was therefore unable to see the beings of love and light which surrounded him at his death.

He was unable to perceive them because he could not absorb what they emanated. When his life on earth fell away from him, he slipped into the realm of death in a state of unconsciousness, a sort of numb sleep.

He only woke up from this unconscious state at a later point. The expression 'the realm of the dead' refers to the lower astral world. This is the spiritual world where there is no light, because people and beings in this lower astral world do not radiate any.

After our death, we all go in the first place to the realm to which we inherently belong, depending on how aware we have become. As no awareness had developed in the rich man, he ended up in the lower astral world where there is no light and there are only other beings like himself: focused on themselves: alone and dark.

Subsequently the story tells how this rich man felt the torments of this realm of the dead. These words in the Bible have led to the greatest misunderstandings, particularly in later centuries when people no longer understood their meaning. The words conjured up images of a hell where fire burns eternally and where people suffer agonies of pain. But this is not what is meant at all. The 'torments' of the rich man are described as a sense of his tongue being on fire – which is why he asks if Lazarus can cool his tongue with some water. What is the meaning of this?

It means – as indicated before – that the man was addicted to eating and drinking. During his lifetime on earth these were his passion and his greatest delight. But now that he has put aside his physical body, he can no longer surrender to this passion. Nevertheless, his desire for food and drink have remained in him: this has been imprinted on his astral body, his soul. So there he is, full of a burning desire to eat and drink, but without a physical body with which he can fulfil this need. We need only recall the descriptions by George Ritchie (see chapter 3) of people in our own time who apparently experience the same thing. This burning desire is actually what is meant by the word 'torments'. And that is what the rich man means when he says: 'for I am tormented in this flame'. You could simply say that this man is suffering from withdrawal symptoms.

Lazarus dwells in the sphere to which he belongs: the high realm of light. The rich man now wants Lazarus to 'descend' from this realm of light to the lower astral world to relieve his pain. But Abraham says that it is not possible to simply descend from the world of light into the lower astral world. Just as it is impossible to simply 'climb-up' into the world of light from the lower astral world.

The rich man then asks for his five brothers on earth to be warned so that they will at least be spared his fate in the realm of death. It is not for nothing that this reference is to five brothers: the number five represents the five senses or sensory organs. Our 'senses' must be transformed, ennobled, spiritualised, so that the spirit in us can come to light and so we can acquire the awareness that enables us to rise to the world of light when we die.

Abraham's answer is that the brothers on earth already have access to 'Moses and the prophets'. This means that they know the (divine) law, given by Moses, and how this should be explained and applied to daily life on earth. The return of somebody from the realm of death will not enable our 'senses' to go through this transformation process. This will only happen if we consciously adopt divine laws in our lives, make it real in the way we live.

It is a wonderful story which Jesus Christ tells us here on the basis of His own observations. Listening and interpreting carefully we can start to hear all sorts of *information* about the spiritual world reflected in this story. And yet Jesus Christ was not so much concerned with passing on this information. He was particularly concerned with quite another aspect: the way in which we live here on earth determines the life that we have after our death. The choice about our after-death life is made now, in this earthly life. Jesus really wants to say that we should be aware that this life is either a path in which our consciousness can grow step by step, or one in which we can descend to a state of unconsciousness, like the rich man. Anyone who opts for the first chooses to develop true love in an open-minded, unconditional, unselfish way.

The story about the rich man and the poor man is often called a parable. However, this is not what it says in the original text. In fact, it is not a parable, but as we said before, a story in which Jesus Christ himself tells about His observations in the spiritual world. However, as the secret knowledge about the spiritual world and about life which continues after death is no longer understood, the story has come to be described as a parable.

We might ask why Jesus Christ is not clearer about what He sees and knows of this spiritual world and life after death. Why does He pass this knowledge and these insights on in the form of a story which can easily be seen as a parable? We have already said that there are two reasons for this. Jesus Christ, like all other masters, only openly discussed this secret knowledge in the intimate circle of his disciples, and not in public. In this respect, He adopted the ancient mystery tradition which had made this distinction for centuries.

The second reason for Jesus Christ's reticence is that He wished to avoid a discussion about whether or not it is possible to clairvoyantly observe the secrets of the spiritual world. A discussion on this question would move the attention away from what He wanted to teach people: that our life here on earth entails a choice. His message here is: we have a choice about how we live and which road we wish to follow: the road of growing awareness, of love and insight, or the road of increasing unconsciousness, sensuality, power, wealth, and a focus on one self.

This to Jesus Christ is the fundamental question everyone is confronted with in his or her life. In this respect, he connected seamlessly with the teachings of Buddha, who also saw life on earth as a road. All sorts of knowledge about the spiritual world and about life after death can be found in biblical texts, as in this story about the rich man and the poor man. This knowledge is there for anyone who has become sensitive to it, for those who have 'ears to hear' as Jesus often said.

Besides the more external aspect of a story, you can also listen to the words behind the words, to what comes through them, to that which is hidden in apparently simple words and stories. Suddenly you become aware of all sorts of other insights which are illuminated. For example such texts from Paul when he talked about death:

It is sown a natural body; it is raised a spiritual body.[3]

Another rather simpler image is:

… knowing that shortly I must put off this my tabernacle …[4]

A beautiful image. The tabernacle is only a shell, protection. This is exactly what our physical body is: it protects the eternal spirit in us. These are only a few examples which can easily be supplemented by others. They may be sufficient for now to demonstrate that biblical texts say much more about death and life after death than people often think.

Notes

1   Luke 16:19-31,
2   For an explanation of the symbolism of 'the bosom of Abraham' and 'the five brothers', see: *Metaphysical Bible Dictionary* Unity Books 1995
3   I Corinthians 15:44
4   2 Peter 1:14.

5. Seven Steps to the World of Light

Death is your birthright.
It is a gift
to which everyone has a right.
It is a resting place for those who are tired,
a refuge for those who have been persecuted.
A lesson for those who have lost the way
A milestone for the pilgrim
And a paradise for believers.

Sai Baba

What happens when we die? What experiences will we have? What life awaits us? These questions will be explored in this chapter. But before we do so we would first like to answer another question. In previous chapters we spoke about the spirit in us which is eternal and which is clothed in three bodies during our life here on earth. The question is: How do I experience this spirit? How do I get in touch with it? What is the difference between my ordinary self and my spiritual self?

My 'ordinary' self, my ego or my lower 'self', manifests in the way I think, what I do, how I talk or how I am wrapped up in myself. I have been given a particular character and the various forces of the planets are revealed in this character, contributing to the quality of my astral body. In my everyday life I therefore have more to do with my soul, my astral body or my ego than with the spirit which is deeply hidden in me. Nevertheless, I can experience this spirit – for example when I meditate and sense an intense peace raising me above time for a short while, above everyday life and ordinary thought. When I experience this (very occasionally) I know that the silent forces of the spirit flow through me for a short while.

The same can happen to me when I am walking in the mountains or in the woods. Suddenly all my everyday thoughts and concerns fall away from me for a moment and I feel at one with nature. It even seems as though I am no longer I, but am in everything : I am these mountains, the air, I am the strength of the mountains, the sparkling fresh air. Even during this experience, I become aware that for just a moment my (lower) self has fallen silent to create room for the spirit within me. These are very rare moments, to be cherished because they remind me of the fact that I am so much more, so much greater than my everyday self, which is so often submerged in responsibilities, worries, duties and challenges.

The spirit in us can break through our ego much more easily when we try to live a life of love, trust and surrender. In that case, my ego will vibrate in a way that is related to the much higher vibration of the spirit in me. However, if my inner self focuses entirely on possessions, on wealth, on myself, my ego will become so hard that it becomes impossible for the spirit to break through this armour. When I manage to focus on honesty, simplicity and compassion, and try to be sensitive and empathise with others, my ego will become increasingly transparent and so more accessible for the inner spirit. Therefore the awareness of the spirit in me is only possible if I opt for a philosophy which does not focus only on myself, but also on God, on other people, the earth and on nature.

This explanation may help to show why the rich man in the last chapter remained or had become unaware in his life after death, while poor Lazarus had perception and awareness. This was related to the different attitudes which they adopted in life. It is also shown in the words of Jesus in the *Gospel According to St. Thomas*:

If you gain what is in yourself,
what you have will save you.
If you do not have it in yourself,
what you do not have will kill you.[1]

'Gaining what is in yourself' refers to the spirit in us, which we can bring to light as we go through our lives. When this spirit in us comes to light and becomes a conscious strength in us, this strength will serve as a light to guide us through the ethereal and astral world to the world of light after the death of our body. But if this spirit in us has become quite impossible to find because our ego has become too hard, and we are not aware of this, there will be no light to guide us to the world of light when our body has died. In this case we will remain 'hanging' in the dark astral world, or the realm of the dead, as it is described in Bible, just like the rich man.

Therefore 'what you do not have (what you have not acquired), will kill you, or will keep you imprisoned in the dark astral world in which you descend in your lack of consciousness. Therefore this concerns a *spiritual* death. Both the biblical and the spiritual, gnostic texts consider that this spiritual death is much more serious than the death of the body.

We will now move on to the real subject of this chapter: What happens when our (physical) body dies? The journey from the material world to the spiritual world can also be seen as a journey in seven stages.

1. View of the other side

When we are dying, our higher self (or spirit), our soul (astral body) and life forces (ethereal body) start to separate from our physical body. However, until death comes, these three remain joined to our physical body by the 'silver cord'.

Perhaps you have experienced people in their dying process, who started on their journey to the other side.

Very often the first sign is that a person's feet and legs go cold as though all life has withdrawn from them. That is in fact what is happening: the withdrawal of the astral and ethereal bodies

But when the ethereal and astral bodies release themselves from the physical body, one becomes clairvoyant. Being clairvoyant actually means that one's ethereal and astral body are more loosely connected with the physical body than in other people. That is why children often have clairvoyant experiences. In them the ethereal and astral bodies are not yet as securely attached to the physical body as they are in adults.

Perhaps this shows why so many people have such beatific experiences at the final boundary, when they are dying. At that moment they become clairvoyant and see real beings in the world of spirit who surround them – both angels and loved ones who have died and who are waiting for them. They hear the music – some speak of a choir of angels – which can be heard in the spiritual world.

Incidentally, light is energy, movement, sound. All forms of energy radiate their own sound. As long as we are in our body we cannot hear this, but as soon as the restrictions of the body begin to fall away, these harmonious sounds become audible to us.

Everyone can have these blissful experiences at the boundary between life and death. But those who have not prepared for this inwardly in some way can remain in darkness. This preparation is

A CHRISTIAN BOOK OF THE DEAD

basically very simple: anyone who has experienced the slightest feeling of true love in this life will have this experience. It is only those who have focused entirely on themselves and who have never seen anyone other than themselves who will not be able to see their spiritual environment.

People who die suddenly can also have this experience. Remember that there are people who have had a near-death experience for only half a minute or even a few seconds and who nevertheless saw their whole lives pass before them. For this brief period they lived outside time, in a timeless space, and therefore had 'all the time in the world' to thoroughly experience their whole life.

2. Breaking the silver cord

Death comes when the silver cord which links the physical body to the ethereal body, the astral body and the higher self is severed irreversibly (rather than partially as during sleep or clairvoyant perception): once the cord is severed, the physical body will not be able to regain life.

This silver cord is rather like the umbilical cord which connects a baby to its mother, usually cut by the doctor or midwife. The silver cord is cut by the angels who have the special task of helping people in their transition to the other side. You may be familiar with this feeling from your own experience: in the presence of someone who is dying, you can be filled with a sense of deep and intense awe. This awe is not only evoked because we find ourselves face to face with death, one of the greatest secrets of life, , but also because we unconsciously absorb the vibration of the angels who are helping someone to cross to the other reality.

These angels carry out all sorts of cosmic laws which have to be obeyed so that the physical body can be separated. These laws

38

are still secret. During the course of evolution they will probably be revealed to us gradually, in stages.

This striking correspondence between the umbilical cord and the silver cord shows that there is good deal of similarity between birth and death. In our human experience, birth and death are two extremes; it is hardly possible to think of a greater contrast. Birth is accompanied by feelings of joy and gratitude, while death evokes feelings of intense sadness and pain. Yet this contrast is an illusion, because birth is also a death: we bid farewell to the spiritual world and leave it behind to enter the material, human world. Death is also a birth: the person who dies leaves the world of embodied people and the material world, but is born into the spiritual world.

3. The film of life

As soon as we have let go of the physical body, we acquire a view of the life we have just completed, in panoramic images. It is rather like looking through a photograph album that contains life and movement: one image after another passes by. The film does not start with our birth, but runs backwards: it starts with taking leave and with death, and then runs back to our birth.

Looking back we also see all sorts of situations we had forgotten about long ago or which we have suppressed from our consciousness. Every life has its dark pages of course, and, alongside joyous times, we are not spared these dark images when we see the film of our life unfold. This film is an objective series of images of the life we have just completed.

During this process, when in fact the ethereal body is slowly though irreversibly separating from the physical, we are still closely linked to our body and to the loved ones we have just left. We are also still very receptive to the feelings of those whom we have left behind. Therefore it is very good for us to find that the people who have remained behind think of us with love and respect. This love can be a great strength and support when the film of our lives passes before us, especially as we look at the darker scenes that we might prefer to skip.

This is why many cultures attach great importance to watching over the body when a person has died. The love and warmth we radiate to the person who died surrounds her[2] and is a real help and strength for her journey.

The memory of the life on earth that has just been completed is stored in our ethereal body, which is the seat of memory. But as we watch this film in the first three days after death, this memory is at the same time imprinted on our astral body. When the ethereal body separates fully and is shed after about three days, we still have the memory of the life that was completed, now stored in our astral body.

Many people feel the person who died still very close to them for the first three days. In fact, she *is* still very close, because the ethereal world is an extension of the material world. As we know, a person's hair and nails continue to grow for three days or so after death, which is a function of the ethereal, life body. It is only when the person who died has also shed her ethereal body that she can enter the astral world and removes herself further from the physical realm.

4. Kamaloka or purgatory

When the ethereal or life body has been left behind after death, after about three days, we enter kamaloka, or purgatory as it is known in the Christian tradition.

We should not conceive of this 'place' in terms of time or space, because these only apply to life on earth. Kamaloka is more a state of consciousness. At this stage we again experience the life we have just completed on earth, and again this review starts with the end of our life on earth and slowly returns to the beginning, to our birth.

However, unlike the first look back at our lives after death, when everything unfurled before us as images or a film from our own point of view, we now see our life from a different perspective. Reviewing each moment when we said or did something, we not only feel what we then felt ourselves, but also what people around us felt. We experience how our words and our actions affected them, deep in their hearts. In this way we become aware of what we really emanated and what this did to the people around us. So it is no longer possible to deceive ourselves that we meant well and therefore couldn't help hurting other people. Kamaloka gives us a naked, honest view of who we were, how we lived and how we affected other people.

At this stage we also become aware of our addictions. Think of the rich man in the Bible who, in our interpretation, became painfully aware of his addiction to food and drink. The impossibility of feeding this addiction forced him into withdrawal and gave him the sense that his tongue was on fire.

As we mentioned, another word for kamaloka is 'purgatory'. Unfortunately, purgatory has often been conceived as a place where we have to atone for our sins, and where we will suffer pain and fire. This is a bleak view, resulting from loss of understanding that fire was meant symbolically, as a description of the withdrawal symptoms which we suffer there.

Purgatory is certainly a place of purification, but it is also a place in which we come to *our own judgement* about the life we have lived. It becomes clear that it is *we* who judge, no one else. We do this by experiencing what *others* felt in response to our words and deeds. Only in this way we can grow in wisdom, insight and love. Therefore, if we wish to use the term purgatory for this period of reflection, it is important to correct all the alienating ideas which the word evokes.

5. Plan for the next life

This intense and painful look back at our lives in kamaloka therefore shows us all sorts of things about ourselves. We see our blind spots, the mistakes we repeated again and again, but we also see ways in which we were good to other people without knowing it. So there are two aspects of this process of looking back: first of all we discover what we can still improve in ourselves, what we still have to learn and what our blind spots are, which we were never fully enough aware of during our life on earth.

At the same time this awareness naturally leads to a powerful impulse to remedy the harm we caused in the world, to others, and thus to a kind of plan for a next life: the next time we descend to the material plane and earthly life, these are the things we will particularly have to work on. Therefore, as we look back, we also start to envisage and plan the conditions we will need to encounter in order to correct our failings. And the angels give us all the help we need to do so.

But we can also make our own what we have *gained* from the life we have just completed. We become aware of this in the form of an increase in love and insight, and can internalise it. What we have gained leads to inner growth which we can take with us forever. At the end of this process of reflection, and internalisation of the spiritual gain we accrue from life, we also leave the astral body behind us. At last the inner spirit is released into its purer form and starts to shine.

For some people, this process of reflection in kamaloka will be completed more quickly than for others. People who have already started to look at themselves critically here on earth will complete this more quickly than those who have been used to blaming others when things go 'wrong'. We can therefore prepare for this transition by practising self-reflection now, during this life.

Through this process of reflection in kamaloka it also becomes clear how much help and guidance we received every night from our own guardian angel. Whether or not we are aware of it, we undergo preparation each night in the spiritual world for the next stages of life awaiting us. Many of our dreams are actually nothing other than the semi-conscious, misty perceptions of this guidance. In kamaloka we gain a clear insight into this guidance, of what we did with it, and how far we were able to realise it.

6. Entering the world of light

Once we have finally discarded the last layer, the astral body, and our inner spirit is finally released, we become a figure of light, liberated like a butterfly from a cocoon. This radiates a magnificent spiritual light and is breathtakingly beautiful. If we were to see this being in front of us now, we would fall to our knees in awe before its radiant beauty.

At this stage, after kamaloka, we leave the astral world and enter the heavenly world of light, or devachan, which consists of many dimensions, usually known as 'spheres'. We can see these as a series of ascending spheres that become increasingly beautiful and light-filled.

Jesus also refers to the fact that the world of light consists of many spheres when he says:

In my Father's house are many mansions.[3]

The original Greek apparently means: 'There are many stepping places on the way to my Father's presence.' When we enter this world of light, we go to the sphere whose intensity is the same as the light which we carry in ourselves. This is often a higher sphere than the sphere in which we lived before we previously descended to earth, for each life is an opportunity to learn and develop love.

When we enter this sphere of light, it is a very joyful occasion: everyone who returns is received enthusiastically and with great joy. We come across all sorts of people here (perhaps they should be referred to as beings of light), and immediately feel very close to them, for they have just as much light in them as we have ourselves. Therefore this arrival in our own sphere is also a celebration of recognition.

7. Living and working in the world of light

In the world of light we continue to work, grow, and relate to those around us, though we are no longer such separate entities as we were on earth. We are embedded in a whole, weaving context of light and life, and have intense community – really being intimately connected to the other beings in our particular sphere.

In many cases what we take on there as our task is something which developed in us during our life on earth as a quiet desire. Here is one example: a girl died when she was eighteen years old. When her mother came to talk with us about her daughter's passing, we told her that her daughter was now in the world of light, meeting, perhaps looking after and guiding others who had died young. The mother was deeply affected by this remark because while alive her daughter had one great desire: to work with children once she had finished her training. The desire which had grown in her during her life on earth, but could not be realised because she passed on so young, was now being fulfilled in the spiritual world.

We often have desires and dreams which we are unable to achieve here on earth, simply because we have to deal with many 'mundane' matters – such as efforts to earn a living or raise our families. But what may remain a quiet desire here on earth can become reality in the world of light.

For example, in the spiritual world we may be able to study, design new ideas for life on earth, or accompany people from lower or higher astral spheres in their growth towards light. We can conceive architectural plans, compose music, paint or teach. In fact, anything is possible! Thus if you know the silent desires of those you loved and who have now gone to the spiritual world, you can also form an idea of what they are doing now.

Those who are sufficiently mature and who have achieved a certain degree of wisdom and love can often serve as a guide for loved ones who have remained on earth. We not only have our own guardian angels who help us and support us on our path through this life, we also may have one or more guides, loved ones who have died who can guide us through earthly life and the spiritual world. Many people are intuitively aware of such loving guidance.

After spending a longer or shorter period in the world of light (since there is no time in the spiritual world, we can only describe this world from our earthly perspective), a desire starts to grow in us to develop further spiritually, so as to be able to enter a higher light sphere. This growth can only really take place on earth.

As this desire grows in us we almost automatically start on our descent to earth. One by one we 'put on' the various layers which prepare us for our new birth on earth: first, the astral body, then the ethereal body, and finally we enter a body growing in a mother's womb. During this journey, the way back to earth, we enter 'the river of forgetfulness' as Plato said, so that we finally arrive back on earth without a clear memory of where we have been, and once more start to get to grips with the earthly, material plane. Living in a new body, we start our next lessons of life.

Notes

1   From the *Gospel According to St. Thomas*
2   To avoid the awkwardness of using both male and female forms, we will alternate from chapter to chapter
3   John 14:2

6. What We Give Back

From what has been so far stated we can see that the purpose of our life on earth is to grow spiritually, developing insight and the strength of love, and increasingly manifesting divine spirit.

We can learn many things during our life on earth, but the most important aspect in this context, as we saw in the last chapter, is simply to become a separate individual, in other words, to develop our own self-awareness. To do this we actually need the encumbrances of the material world. In the spiritual world we cannot develop self-awareness, because there we are not separated from each other. In the spiritual world we live as spiritual beings in each other, in a state of shared consciousness – a state which we can hardly imagine with ordinary, everyday consciousness. It is only because we have our own physical body on earth that we are divided from each other here and can become independent individuals with a separate 'I' and our own consciousness.

In the last chapters we saw that in addition to a physical body we also have an ethereal body which permeates our physical body with life energy. In addition, we need an astral body because it is only this that gives us our own soul, our own inner world. And we have an 'I' in order to be able to develop our own personality and our own consciousness, including our self-awareness.

The 'I' consists of a 'lower' and a 'higher' aspect. The lower is particularly rooted in the astral body, and influenced by it. It forms our personality. The higher aspect comprises our spiritual being. This spiritual being, the spiritual self, mainly lives unconsciously in the depths of the soul, and also in the unconscious impulses that often lead us, as though by an unseen hand, to the tasks and people we need in life – to everything we can call our 'destiny'.

We saw that on starting the return journey to earth for a new incarnation we put on these bodies one by one. These bodies derive from different spheres. The astral body from the astral world or the world of the soul, the ethereal body from the living, weaving, ethereal world, and the physical body from the world of physical matter, which we 'put on' in our mother's womb.

After death, we relinquish these bodies again, and they return to the different spheres to which they belong. The physical body we leave behind is buried or cremated, the matter which remains going back to the earth. After death, the ethereal body is reabsorbed by the ethereal world, and later the astral body also returns to the astral or soul world.

But these bodies which, as it were, we 'borrow' for a while from the spiritual world, change as a result of our use of them. In other words, at death they are not the same anymore as the bodies we received on our way down to earth. We have lived in them and experienced life through them, and so changed them in a positive or in a negative sense.

By growing spiritually and developing awareness and love, we add positive forces to these bodies. This new consciousness and the increase in loving forces will continue to have a positive effect after death in the various worlds to which these bodies return. If we have pursued only the external things of life and concentrated on baser desires, this will also be assimilated in those worlds, having a disruptive effect in physical, ethereal and astral realms.

What does all this mean? It shows that the quality of our lives not only affects earthly reality and our own narrow sphere, but also the vast spheres of spiritual worlds, and therefore the whole human and cosmic community!

This shows that the choices we make – or fail to make – during our life on earth have very far-reaching consequences, much further and greater than we realise.

7. The House of the Spirit

We live on earth to develop our individuality, or in other words: to develop in our 'I', in our personality, the forces of our spiritual self. In each new life on earth we work on ourselves to reveal something more of the divine centre in us.

This working on ourselves can be compared to building and then inhabiting a house.

A house on earth is built with earthly materials: stone, cement, wood etc. What the house is to be like, in other words its design and the architectural plans, are drawn up in the architect's office. The house of our body is built on earth but the design and the structural plan must be sought with the divine beings in the spiritual world. Incidentally, this is why God is sometimes referred to as the Supreme Architect of the Universe.

When we have completed a life on earth, our divine core, the inhabitant of the house, must always return to the spiritual world to consult the divine beings and the spiritual building plan and find new strength and inspiration for further work in the physical world, just as a building contractor will constantly return to the plans, and discuss them with the architect.

So when, after every life on earth, we return to the spiritual world, we look back at the life we have just lived and see what we have become, comparing this with the original plan or drawings to find out what still needs to be done...

The design for the next life, with all its tasks and requirements, is based on this. In this way we work slowly towards perfection in each of our lives on earth.

How does our spiritual self or divine centre actually develop in us on earth? Our higher self is part of the spiritual world of light and consists of, in fact *is*, consciousness, wisdom and love. It develops in us when we become conscious of things, acquire insights and knowledge and develop warmth and love that we show in our actions. The more we do so the more the strength of our higher self, of our divine centre, works in us and manifests itself through us.

This high aim, the development of the spark of God in us, starts with very simple tasks in daily life on earth, in the material world. Even something as ordinary as driving a car is part of this. When I am driving, I constantly have to be alert, i.e., conscious of myself. I not only have to know where I am driving to, but I must find the way and drive without causing any accidents or making too many detours. In addition, I constantly have to take other drivers, cycles and pedestrians into account.

All of our daily life is full of these sorts of unnoticed exercises and opportunities. They awaken us, for they give us insight into ourselves, our own behaviour, the behaviour and needs of other people and the way we deal with them. In the spiritual world these exercises do not exist. We only find them on earth. Only the world of matter provides the resistance we need to awaken.

So it would be wrong to think that because something is 'mundane' (literally 'of the world') it is of little consequence, and that spiritual development only follows from lofty thoughts and ideals. The real practice of awareness needs the ordinary situations of daily life.

People who have had near-death experiences can tell us a lot about such growth of knowledge and love. For example, they frequently tell us that the figure of light whom they encountered on the other side showed them that life is all about two things: learning to love other people, and acquiring knowledge and insight.[1] Knowledge and insight into oneself, life, other people, the development of the cosmos.

Such knowledge and insight does not have to mean knowing all sorts of learned facts, but knowledge based on insight. Knowledge based on insight makes us whole and therefore enables us to achieve true human understanding. This sort of knowledge can only be acquired if it is not limited to the intellect, rational thinking, but is also connected with feelings and the heart. When that happens knowledge becomes an inner experience of truth, which is the spirit self's substance.

The following story illustrates this. One theologian who had a near-death experience told a researcher that he had seen what an arrogant fellow he was with all his theology and the way in which he looked down on people who were not members of his Church and did not have the same theological views as he did. The figure of light with whom he looked back at his life appeared to be completely uninterested in his theology. The theologian explained:

> In fact, he seemed to find it rather amusing, because he had no interest at all in the Church of which I am a member. He wanted to know what was going on in my heart, not what was going on in my head.[2]

In other words, pure intellectual, rational knowledge is of no importance at all after death. What remains is what you have experienced, understood in a deeper sense and what you have consciously added to your heart.

One woman who had a near-death experience describes that everything she had achieved, seen externally, everything she had owned and knew as an external fact, disappeared in the presence of the spiritual being of light. However, she said:

On the other hand, the acts in which I had shown any unselfish love and an interest in my fellow human beings, were glorified and laid down forever in the register of my life, no matter how fleeting or insignificant those moments might have been.[3]

The fusion of insight, knowledge and love, which allows the strength of the spiritual self to increase in us, is perfectly expressed by the woman we quoted in chapter 3. We would like to repeat her words once again:

But since I died, all of a sudden, right after my experience, I started wondering whether I had been doing the things I had done because they were good, or because they were good for *me*. Before, I just reacted off the impulse, and how I run things through my mind first, nice and slow. Everything seems to have to go through my mind and be digested first.

I try to do things that have more meaning, and that makes my mind and soul feel better. And I try not to be biased, and not to judge people. I want to do things because they are good, not because they are good to me. And it seems the understanding I have of things now is so much better. [4]

This woman's experiences of the spiritual world and the process of consciousness which followed them led to her spiritual awakening. From then on she questioned her own motives and first had, as she says, to 'assimilate and digest everything' in her spirit. This is the process of knowledge which leads to insight, and this insight means that she wants to 'do the right thing' in a much more conscious way. Doing good out of your own will and consciousness is the strength of love in a real spiritual sense, and has a good and healing effect on other people, on herself, and also, ultimately on the whole earth.

All this awakens people and lets them develop the forces of the spiritual self in their 'I'.

Notes

1   See: Raymond Moody: *Life After Life*
2   Quoted in Moody: *The Light Beyond*
3   Charles P. Flynn: *After the Beyond: Human Transformation and the Near-Death Experience*
4   Raymond Moody: *Life After Life*

8. Body, Soul and Spirit

Before we examine from another perspective the path we take, after death, through the various regions of the spiritual world, let us just look briefly again at the interrelationship between spiritual being, soul and physical body.

The soul and the 'I' draw our spirit or divine centre from the spiritual world into the physical world so that it can have the necessary experiences in that world. For only through experiences in the world of matter can we become self-aware and develop. We can experience things on earth because there are all sorts of forces at work in our soul and in our 'I' : feelings of sympathy and antipathy, joy and sorrow, passions, desires, needs, impulses, wishes etc.

Our soul lives in a powerful interaction with the body and all its processes. You will discover this very clearly when tired or ill. Because your soul is linked so closely to the physical body you experience tiredness and illness as a painful or unpleasant feeling in your soul, identifying with it: *I* feel unwell or dreadful. The same is true in reverse: if you feel painfully affected by a particular experience this will eventually come to expression in your body.

This close link between body and soul is very fundamental for the way in which we live and experience ourselves. As we have seen, though, the soul is a kind of mediating bridge between body and spirit or higher self, and the traffic flows in two directions: we experience many things as a result of the movement of the spirit in the soul. Some thoughts fill our soul with joy, others with disgust. If we do something well, or something good, this is experienced as a pleasant feeling in the soul.

The woman quoted in the last chapter described how she felt better in her spirit and her soul when she tried to do things which were meaningful. Sense and meaning are elements which relate to the spirit. For example, if you gain a deeper insight into yourself or into a relationship with another person because you suddenly see the meaning in it, this will primarily give you a sense of joy and gratitude in your soul and in your higher self. You can suddenly become aware that this gives your life its sense and meaning.

Such awareness of a deeper level of meaning is the growth of the spirit in us.

Some people are wholly taken up by their physical existence. They don't think much about deeper things, but are largely out to profit as much as possible and acquire all sorts of material goods: a new kitchen every few years, or new furniture for the house because the neighbours have it. It is clear that their soul and 'I' are wholly absorbed by the physical world. And because of that their spirit is drawn completely into this sphere too, so that, in a certain sense, their spirit becomes trapped in the physical world. The result is that such people lose their vision and sense of why they are on earth.

On the other hand, difficult problems that people meet in life often bring them to ask important questions that help them further. What is life really all about? What is the meaning of my life? Why do I meet all this?

Often, after a certain time, they come to a particular insight, and then start to do things differently, or organise their lives in a different way.

The woman quoted in the previous chapter is an example of this development. When this questioning and searching happens it shows that the spirit self is no longer fully submerged in the physical world, but begins to awaken. That is why people who have conquered difficult situations in their lives, can be inwardly strong. Through working through that hardship, they have touched on the inner strength of their spiritual self and that has opened something of its source.

The way spirit, soul and body interrelate is different in different people. We will now examine how this can influence and affect life after death.

9. The Path Through Spirit Realms

Looking back from the ethereal world

We described earlier how we put aside the physical body at the moment of death and immediately afterwards see our whole life unfurling before us. This is because the ethereal body, where *everything* is stored which we experience and think during our life on earth, is now released and can reveal its contents to us in images. After three days these images fade, and looking back in this way comes to an end. This fading means that the ethereal body is dissolving and returning to the ethereal world.

Looking back in the astral world or world of the soul

During our life on earth our astral body is compressed and confined. When we enter the astral world, the astral body begins to open up and return to the astral world from which it was formed. The compressed shape starts to flow, and when it opens up all that was taken up in this astral body during our life on earth stands before us unconcealed and vibrant.

It is now that we start to relive the life which has just been completed from the point of view of others who were affected by us, both in positive and negative ways. The whole process, which takes quite a long time – approximately one third of the life that has ended – means that we acquire a true and objective image of ourselves in our own life in a way different from the 'film' revealed by the ethereal world.

At the same time, these images evoke desire in us to do things better and differently in the next life.

When the astral body opens up, we have arrived in the astral world or world of the soul. Before we explore the world of the soul we will, for the sake of clarity, list the various levels of the spiritual world,. These are based on knowledge which Rudolf Steiner gained from his spiritual investigations:[1]

1. The ethereal world.
2. The lower and higher astral world or world of the soul.
3. Devachan, or the 'lower' and the 'higher' world of light. In the Christian tradition, this lower and higher world of light is also known as 'Paradise' or the heavenly world.
4. The highest divine world.

As described earlier, the astral world or world of the soul is concerned in the first place with processing earthly experiences. This is achieved, after death, by experiencing your life again – this time through the souls of the people you encountered in life. Reliving your experiences in this way will evoke all sorts of feelings and emotions such as joy and gratitude, but also sorrow and pain for what you have done to others, often unconsciously, by your words, deeds or omissions. At the same time the world where you are now, and the spiritual beings of light, the angels, who support you in the process of reliving your life, give you insight into how things could have been done better.

We may feel pain when we realise it is not possible to make good our failings now, but that we have to wait for the next life.

Reliving every experience and gaining the subsequent insights and intentions to do things differently in the future, means we can work through our earthly experiences. As a result of this reliving of our life and these insights, we learn, and gain wisdom. This means that our divine core is increasingly liberated.

In addition to working through the life that has come to an end, one of the important things in the astral world or world of the soul is, as we said before, to learn to deal with the loss of the physical body. As we no longer have this physical body, we cannot fulfil all sorts of passions, needs, longings and desires, though these forces are still fully active in the soul after death, which initially remains focused on physical existence.

Only slowly do we readjust and turn away to a different kind of existence.

In the astral or soul world we are purified or cleansed of the desires and influences linked with physical existence and acquire an insight into what is essential and what is not. Only then can we enter higher regions of the spiritual world, the world of light. Our divine centre is liberated to the extent that we work through our experiences in the world of the soul when we have died, come to an insight and pass through the process of extinguishing these desires and needs. 'Liberated' here means that our spirit itself increasingly opens up its own spiritual forces.

How does this journey through the various regions of the astral world take place? In trying to describe the journey through various regions of the astral world or world of the soul, one immediately encounters the difficulty that our words mainly relate to the physical, material world, where they have been coined. The world of the soul is completely different, subject to different laws so that we lack a way to describe and express this other world. Anything we say about spiritual realms, therefore, is at best just through metaphors, is a hinting at qualities that cannot be grasped in earthly concepts.

So when we refer to different layers or areas in the world of the soul, we should not imagine that these exist one above the other, but *in* one another. They merge and permeate each other. One area after another opens up to you to the extent that you have the necessary qualities and abilities, or start to acquire these as you pass through them. You must have an inner affinity to a sphere or area of the spiritual world for it to open up to you. Your life on earth and the spiritual and soul forces which you may or may not have developed there determine your life in the spiritual world after death: which areas open up to you and which remain closed and how long you remain in them.

In addition, you live *simultaneously* in different areas with different parts of your soul. With those parts of your soul which are still not liberated, you remain in the 'lower' areas, particularly to begin with. Those aspects of your soul in which your spirit on earth was already liberated to some extent, live in the higher areas of the soul world. If you did not develop spiritually on earth and were completely absorbed by external material things, you will (initially) spend an important part of your time in the lower world of the soul in your life after death, engaging in processes of 'purification'.

The seven regions of the world of the soul

The astral world or the world of the soul is subdivided into seven regions or areas. Rudolf Steiner named and described these regions as follows:[2]

1. The region of the glow of desire
2. The region of fluid openness to impressions
3. The region of desires
4. The region of likes and dislikes
5. The region of the light of the soul
6. The region of the active force of the soul
7. The region of the real life of the soul

The first four regions are sometimes referred to as the *lower world of the soul*, because a person is still focused largely on desires and the physical world at this level. The fifth, sixth and seventh regions comprise the *higher world of the soul*, because the soul is already more purified and the spirit is able to manifest itself more clearly at this level.

The lower astral worlds

1. *The region of the glow of desire* is the lowest region in the world of the soul. We will be attracted to this if we spent our life focusing on the lowest drives and desires related to the physical body. Those who die without carrying any of these desires will pass through this condition without noticing it, because they have no connection with it.

   The region of the glow of desire is a dark state in the world of the soul where our burning desires are slowly eroded. Therefore it is a state of suffering. Nevertheless, this purifying suffering should not be seen in the same sense as the suffering in the physical world. After a while, the person starts to desire purification because he feels that eradicating these desires is the only way of reducing the suffering and the imperfection related to it, and the only way to progress.

2. *The region of fluid openness to impressions* is the second region in the world of the soul. It is related to the time and attention we spent on earth engaged in trivialities and the superficial and transient experience of all sorts of sensory impressions. We live in this condition to the extent that we were affected by these tendencies in our soul.

3. The third region is *the region of desires*. We experience the influence of this region through everything which we carry with us after death, related to wishes and desires focused on

the earth. For example, the things which we still wanted to do or experience there. As these wishes and desires cannot be fulfilled, they slowly die away in this region.

4. The fourth region, *the region of likes and dislikes*, imposes special tests and trials. As we saw in the previous chapter, our body and soul have a strong effect on each other. The body causes pleasant and agreeable feelings or unpleasant emotions and a feeling of dissatisfaction in the soul. During our physical life we experience our body as ourselves. Our sense of self, our ego is based on this. The more strongly we are connected to this body in our soul, the more this applies.

   However, after death, the physical body on which this sense of self is based no longer exists. This means that it is as though we feel eroded in our soul, as though we have lost ourselves. This continues to apply until it has become clear that our true self is not to be found in the physical world, but is a spiritual being. The effects of this fourth area therefore destroy the illusion of the self, in so far as it is based on physical aspects.

   As a result of this process, our soul is cured and purified. Those aspects which strongly connected us to the physical world in the past are now conquered, and therefore we are in a sense liberated from ourselves. While we were predominantly focused on ourselves up to that time, we are now able to open up towards other people who have died, and towards spiritual beings living in the world of the soul, full of empathy.

The higher astral worlds

With the fifth region of the world of the soul, we enter the *higher worlds of the soul*. This brings us closer to the true spiritual world or world of light. This is primarily because our higher self or spiritual self has now been liberated to a greater extent by all these processes. We experience this gradual liberation of our spirit in our soul as an awakening of a creative force of the soul. A force that illuminates everything around us.[3] This leads to a deep sense of happiness and true heavenly wonder.

The higher regions of the world of the soul, regions five, six and seven, particularly open up to us to the extent that we have created the conditions for this during our life on earth. This means the extent to which we had and observed ethical and moral ideas and developed religious feelings and spirituality.

The higher regions will however remain closed to the extent that we led an amoral, asocial, a-religious, or in a deeper sense, an 'unchristian' life during our time on earth. If this is the case, we will not have access to the keys which will open the doors to these regions. In this sense, 'unchristian' at this level does *not* mean that we did not go to church, but that we did not develop sufficient loving forces, forces emanating from Christ.

For those who lack the necessary qualities in the fifth, sixth and seventh regions in the world of the soul, existence during this part of the journey is full of painful solitude: like living in a shell or in a prison from which one cannot escape. Again, we remain in this condition, until we achieve insight into what life is really about and experience this as being true.

However, anyone who does feel at home in these spheres because of the life he has led on earth will be granted the strength for a healthy and powerful astral body and ethereal body in his next life. If you are able to connect with this sphere, the higher spiritual beings inhabiting these regions can make contact with you and grant you their health-giving spiritual forces.[4]

5. The fifth region is *the region of the light of the soul.* As our soul has already been largely liberated from the focus on physical existence after we die, our interest in other things than

ourselves and our own life becomes increasingly strong. Nevertheless, processes of purification also take place here.

The souls of those who have died are related to this fifth region if they were not entirely concerned during their physical lifetime with satisfying their 'lower' desires. but were happy with their environment, such as the natural environment, and were able to enjoy this.

However, it is possible to enjoy nature in different ways. We can enjoy it so that it simply gives us a good feeling and nothing more. Or we can enjoy nature and at the same time take an interest in the way in which the spirit is manifesting itself in nature. In other words, how there is something unchanging and divine in the transience of nature, which becomes tangible and visible and arouses a sense of wonder that fills us with awe and gratitude.

The first way of enjoying nature means that we need purification in this region of the astral world because we restrict ourselves only to the external aspects of nature and use no more than our physical senses to enjoy it.

The second way of being open to nature, puts us in contact with the spirit itself, and in this way becomes a permanent strength in us. This means that no further purification is required in the fifth region because we already carry the spiritual element in us.

If our soul was mainly concerned with feeling good when engaging in religious activities during our life on earth, or if we wished to feel physically better in this way, we will also have to be purified in this region. In fact, we will be made aware of the illusions which this attitude led to on earth.

As in the other regions, we will remain in this region until this desire for the earthly experience of religion has disappeared. In this area we live together with others who had an affinity to nature and religious life in the same way as we, and who related to it in a similar way. This leads to an intense feeling of solidarity.

6. The sixth region is *the region of the active force of the soul*. If we have actively used the capacity for love during our lifetime, this capacity will be strengthened in this region because we are able to absorb the cosmic forces of love radiating towards us from the higher spiritual beings in this area.

The part of the soul which does all sorts of good things without being egoistical, but is nevertheless motivated by the sensory satisfaction resulting from these acts, is purified in this region of the astral world.

For example, many idealists sacrifice themselves in order to achieve a particular ideal. Of course, this is very good in itself, but usually the satisfaction which they experience personally in realising these ideals also plays a part. The same applies for the work created by artists and scientists. This feeling is purified here.

7. In the highest, seventh, region of the soul world, that of *the true life of the soul*, the last vestiges which still connect the soul to the earth are purified. As a soul you now reach the heart of the universe in which Christ unites all of mankind. You feel at one with the universe as a whole, and what you were on earth in the past is now experienced as something external to you.

Nevertheless, some purification is still needed at this level too – the need to transcend all sense that the physical is somehow more substantial than the world of the spirit. Many people, including many scientists, focus their research on processes which relate only to physical reality. Anything which transcends this is considered to be unscientific or rather airy-fairy. Here this belief melts away like snow in the sun and we become aware that everything which can be found on earth originates in the divine world, thus liberating the spirit entirely from its focus on the earth.

We can only identify with and fully perceive this highest soul region if we practised tolerance and absorbed the spiritual element in ourselves on earth, transcending all religions and religious views, and linking people together. In other words, if we have recognised the divine spirit which connects everything and everyone.

Once we have passed through this seventh region our soul has not only completed its task during life on earth, but has also discarded everything which still imprisoned us as a spiritual being. This means that the task of the soul, of the astral body, has been fulfilled. It can now be returned to its own element: the astral or soul world. And so the last vestige of the astral body is discarded.

Enriched by everything that it underwent during the life on earth and by the processes of assimilation and purification in the ethereal and astral world, our spiritual being is now liberated from all restraints and radiates a bright light. We begin to hear the sounds of the spiritual world around us, the music of the spheres. We are raised to still higher regions, where we live in our own intrinsic element - devachan or the heavenly world, also called paradise.

In this 'third world', the devachan, we will not only see and hear these higher beings of light that inhabit the worlds of light, but will also start to work with them. We will become active and creative, helping to develop mankind and the cosmos. This leads to a sense of heavenly joy, harmony, peace and fulfilment which cannot be described in earthly words.

The time in the worlds of light or devachan

Before we can follow the spirit or divine core on its further journey, we should first explore the region in which it now lives: the 'world of the spirit', devachan, also called paradise.

This world is so unlike the physical world, even less so than the soul world, that it can only be described by means of a few hints and suggestions.

For example, Rudolf Steiner pointed out that this world is made of a 'material' of which human thought consists. It is a world of *living* thoughts, or *spiritual beings*. These living thoughts or spiritual beings have also been referred to as *archetypes*, for example, by Plato. These archetypes are creative beings. Everything in this region is in constant active movement. Everything is incessantly creative. There is no rest, things do not stay in one place as they do in the physical world or even to some extent in the soul world.

The situation here can best be described as a *workshop* of thoughts where everything is made which you can experience during your earthly existence. Every stone, every plant or tree, every animal that exists on earth, as well as every person and everything that is achieved in the field of human creativity, originates here, as an archetype or living thought. On earth, this stone, this plant, this tree, this animal, this person or this work of art is 'only' an *image* of archetypal images in this region of the spiritual world. Here you also once more encounter your own physical body, but now as archetype, a living being of thought.

The archetypes are energy, vibration, and sound. They manifest as a purely spiritual phenomenon which cannot be compared to the sounds we hear in the physical world. The beings of the spiritual world express themselves in this spiritual vibration, this sea of sound. Their harmonies, rhythms and melodies sounding together express the basic laws of their existence, their interrelationships and connections. It is clear that

Rittelmeyer, whose journey through the heavenly world was described in chapter 3, was describing this region in the spiritual world when he referred to the 'singing', 'sounding' of the chorus of angels.

The development of our spirit in the heavenly world takes place when we empathise with different regions of this realm. Gradually our own being fuses with the spiritual beings inhabiting these regions and we temporarily assume their qualities. These in turn permeate our own being with their creativity; and in this way grant us their strength so that we can later be active with greater strength on earth.

This means that in these regions of the spiritual world we can exchange the fruits yielded by our own life in return for new spiritual forces and capacities with which we can continue in our next incarnation on earth. The actual preparation for our next life on earth therefore begins here.

We become increasingly aware that we inherently and essentially belong to the spiritual world of light. In oriental Vedantic wisdom this consciousness is expressed by the saying, 'I am Brahma', which means: I am part of the archetypal being that has created all beings.

Like the world of the soul or the astral world, the heavenly world or devachan is also subdivided into different lower and higher regions. The archetypes described above can be found at every level. At succeeding levels, for example, we find archetypal images of the *physical world*, archetypal images of *life*, then archetypal images of everything related to *the soul*. At higher levels spiritual beings give the archetypal images of the lower levels the *impulses for their activity*. This is where we learn about the *intentions* which underlie our world. In what follows we will try to give a general description of these seven levels of the heavenly world, again based on Rudolf Steiner's research and insights.[5]

1. In the *first region*, we encounter everything which determined our physical, earthly circumstances in archetypal form, as a *living* being of thought: our family, the nation into which we were born, the land where we lived, the friends we had, the work we did, etc. We experience all these things again, but this time from an active and spiritual perspective. The love which we felt for our family and the friendship which we showed other people now starts to live in us in a more inward way. Our capacities in this sense become stronger. We are connected to the loving impulses which were the basis for our life and activities on earth. This reaffirmation and strengthening enables us to later re-enter earthly existence as a more advanced human being.

   In this region of the spiritual world we encounter all the people we lived with in the physical world and with whom we had an inner connection. We can continue this shared life in a spiritual way, with mutual love and respect, no longer hampered by all the restrictions attaching to life in the physical world.

2. In the *second region*, we come across the archetypes of life: living beings of thought produced by the living unity present everywhere. On earth the effect of this archetype image is expressed in every form of worship which we feel for the whole of Creation, the cosmos, the unity of mankind or the harmony of the world. *Religious* life on earth comes from this region. The term 'religion' means: re-connection with the great universe, with God. In this region we see the fruits of this religious life and therefore of the life connected to these things – for example the fact that our individual destiny cannot be separated from the community to which we belong. Here we develop the ability to see ourselves as part of a whole. Our consciousness, our religious feelings focused on

purity and truthfulness, are also strengthened in this region. The gift we receive here is to be incarnated with a greater capacity for truth and purity.

In this second region, we are connected with all those with whom we share a common conviction or belief.

One person's near-death experience gives a sense of this second realm:

> I knew them completely just as they knew me completely, without words and without thought. I understood that everyone lived in a state of perfection, harmony and love. We were freed of all those deceptive things which are the cause of wars and other conflicts, according to historians, such as nation, hunger, shelter. These conditions meant that you were in an exceptional state because there was neither any hatred nor any other disruptive emotions. There was only an all-embracing sense of love. This love was so comprehensive that feelings close to it such as consideration, respect, sympathy, interest were all incorporated…everything fused into a single feeling.[6]

Everything we experience in the earlier regions is retained in succeeding regions. Therefore links with family and friends are not broken when we enter the life of the second or of subsequent levels. Again, as we said before, these levels are not separated from each other but present *in* each other. We experience each new region, or it opens up to us, when we have acquired the inner capacities to observe those things we could not see before, even if we were right in their midst.

3. The *third region* of the heavenly world contains archetypal images of the world of the soul. Everything that lives in the world of the soul or the astral world is present here as a living

archetype or being of thought. Everything we did for the community, in unselfish dedication to our fellow human beings when still on earth, bears fruit here. Conversely we can also say that at that time we lived in the inspiration from this third region in devachan.

All those who work to serve the whole community, such as Gandhi, Mother Theresa and Nelson Mandela, have been given the ability to do so in this region. This gift was given them because they developed a special relationship with this region in their previous lives.

4. The *fourth region* contains archetypal images of everything which the human being brings to the world and creates there through his spirit. This level therefore relates to creations and inventions in the arts, sciences and technology, forms of government which are developed and so on. Without the intervention of man there could be no physical expressions of all these things in the physical world of matter. We owe the constant development of mankind on earth to impulses from this fourth region. Conversely, we also bring something back from this region. Everything which people manage to achieve during their life on earth in terms of scientific achievements, technical inventions, artistic ideas and creations, bears fruit in this fourth region and is active there.

This is the region where artists, scholars, and great inventors find their inspiration during their previous time in devachan, so that they are able to contribute to the continuing development of human culture in their next incarnation. This is probably the region which George Ritchie described (see chapter 3) as the region in the spiritual world where discoveries are made, that are later physically realised on earth.

In the higher regions of the heavenly world, the *fifth, sixth and seventh regions*, we ascend to the higher world of light where we can experience the intentions of the spirit in relation to life on earth. In these last three regions or spheres we are bathed in the rays of elevated beings for whom the highest divine beings of divine wisdom and love in the worlds of the Trinity, are clearly visible. These elevated beings in the higher devachan world are also referred to as Seraphim, Cherubim and Thrones.

In these higher regions of the heavenly world we also meet the human spirits with whom we will be connected in the next life on earth.

5. Our true spiritual being and nature is shown most clearly in the time between two incarnations when we ascend to the *fifth region*. Here we exist as true self: the individual being who assumes a different appearance in every incarnation, but who appears as the same intrinsic being in each earthly life. As a spiritual being of light we are in our own element here. The spiritual self takes the fruit of previous lives with it to the next life. It carries with it the consequences and results of former incarnations.

In this fifth region our true self can develop freely in every direction. The strength which we take with us from this region to the next life depends on the extent to which we made connections with this region during our life on earth. If we had an active inner life on earth or tried to achieve the spirit's intentions by means of wise and generous love, we find a special connection with this region.

If, on the other hand, we immersed ourselves in ordinary, everyday life in such an exclusive way that we became concerned only with superficial things, then we will have sown little that can bear fruit in this region; and can therefore be granted little to take from it.

If this is so, our period in this fifth region may give rise to a need to be given such an impulse through special events of fate in our next physical life, in such a way that we cannot avoid developing the qualities and capacities which belong to this region. An example of intervention that achieved this is the near-death experience of the woman described in chapter 3. This experience meant that she first contemplated everything thoroughly and then tried to do the right thing for its own sake. Such attempts gradually lead to the development of the spiritual self. One can also imagine all sorts of hardship which can turn one's focus more inwards and through inner activity develop inner strengths: an example might be Nelson Mandela's long years in prison, from which he emerged as a loving, generous spirit. He must, however, have already had this disposition, for such experiences might otherwise only breed bitterness and hate

In the fifth region we can look back on our own past on earth and feel that everything which we experienced there will be absorbed in the intentions which must be realised in the future in oneself and in humanity as a whole.

This means that in this region we also gain an insight into the great pattern of mankind's evolution, in which we actively participate with our own development.

In addition to this general insight we are also able to look back at our own earlier lives, and forwards in a sort of prophetic way to later incarnations. This means that the divine core develops in us in this region and prepares us to contribute in our next incarnation even more strongly to the high aims the divine beings have in mind in relation to the development of mankind.

6. In the *sixth region* of the heavenly world our deeds relate to everything linked most closely to the true essence of the

world. This means that we are not looking for things that are to our own advantage, but only for what should happen so that the earth and the cosmos can develop as they should.

7. The *seventh region* of the heavenly world leads to the boundary separating the worlds of light from even higher spiritual regions: the highest divine worlds, the regions of the Divine Trinity. In these immeasurable worlds which cannot be described in earthly words, live the highest divine creative forces and forces of love. All beings of the spiritual world, from the lowest to the highest, are at its service.

When you die, your human spirit also goes through these highest divine regions, though unconsciously. The things which live and take place there cannot be consciously understood or even borne in our present stage of human development. In fact, after death, most people do not consciously proceed much further than the third, or at most the fourth region of the heavenly world. Then the light of their consciousness is extinguished and they become blind to what surrounds them. Only a few people who have developed sufficiently far on earth are able to proceed consciously through these higher realms.

Yet now that the spirit is increasingly awakening within mankind during our present evolutionary period – more and more people consciously work on themselves – we can say that gradually more people will reach the fifth level of the heavenly world when they die. This means that in future generations the strength and the effect of the spirit will increase considerably on earth.

The path to a new existence on earth

To summarize: on our path after death we pass through all the levels and regions of the spiritual worlds: the ethereal world, the astral or soul world, the devachan world or paradise, up to the very highest divine worlds of the Trinity. Finally, having 'ascended' into the spirit worlds as far as we can, we become fully cosmic. We have now arrived at the turning point of our existence between death and a new birth, on earth.

At this stage we are ready to return to an earthly human existence.[7] This journey back to earth takes place in the reverse order through all the regions described, of the heavenly world, the astral or soul world and the ethereal world and from there into the physical world of matter.

However, as we return we do not *discard* qualities, possibilities and impulses as we did on our way 'up', but instead *receive* gifts from the spiritual beings who live in each of these regions: not only our the astral body and our 'I', but also our ethereal body and our physical body.

In addition to this, we receive other gifts from them: skills and talents which we can use in our next incarnation. For example, in the third region of the heavenly world or higher devachan we receive the essence of the human capacity for memory; in the second region, the ability to create human thoughts; and in the first region, the spiritual substance which later forms the earthly 'I'. At the same time the spiritual basis for our future physical body is formed in these three spheres.

The quality of these gifts is determined by the quality of what you previously gave back as the 'proceeds' from your past life when you ascended into the spiritual world after death.

On descending through the various levels of the astral or soul world, the archetypal image of our heart is formed in the highest soul region which has a special relationship with Christ. The first contact with the current of heredity is also formed in this region, although we may only be born centuries later. As we descend further into the sixth, fifth region of the soul world, our future destiny is formed, in particular with regard to the family and nation in which we will be born.[8]

The decisive steps towards rebirth are taken when we come down into the four lower regions of the soul world. While our consciousness expanded tremendously in these regions immediately after death, it is now the task of the spiritual beings working there to gradually condense and confine our consciousness into the dreaming consciousness of a baby. This happens during the period when our new physical body is being prepared in the mother's womb.

Notes

[1]   For the description of the different areas of the spiritual world, we made extensive use of Rudolf Steiner's book, *Theosophy*, especially the chapter, 'The Three Worlds'.
[2]   See note 1 above.
[3]   Rudolf Steiner: *Life Beyond Death*
[4]   M. Burckhardt: *Die Erlebnisse nach dem Tod*
[5]   See note 1 above.
[6]   Charles P. Flyn: *After the Beyond: Human Transformation and the Near-Death Experience*
[7]   Stanley Drake: *Though You Die*
[8]   Each nation has particular characteristics and qualities that can develop and extend our own inner being, and so we seek out the nationality, and family, that can best provide the opportunities to grow that we need.

10. *Driven from Paradise for a Second Time*

Nowadays what we experience when we pass through the gateway of death is very different from what we used to experience in former times. Even though we can no longer remember this, we have already died many times in previous lives and have therefore often taken the path through death.

Each time, though, this path was different, just as our life on earth was different on each occasion. Initially, in earlier ages, the door to the world of light was wide open after our death. When we died, therefore, we entered this world of light almost immediately.

But the more we began to feel at home on earth, to inhabit it fully, the more closely bound up with earth we became. The more our earthly self developed, the more difficult it became to return to the world of light. In the end, in fact, this return to the world of light grew impossible, and after our death we became imprisoned in astral worlds instead, caught half way between the world of light and the material world. We began to be reincarnated from this astral world, rather than passing through all the levels described in the previous chapter.

If we want to understand why the path to the world of light became increasingly difficult after death, we first have to explain something about human evolution here on earth. This development on earth is intimately connected with what we experience after our death.

The first book of the Bible, Genesis, starts with an impressive description of the creation of the earth, life on earth and the creation of man. This is immediately followed by a dramatic description of the fate of the first human beings, Adam and Eve, which tells us how this first couple were driven from paradise. In paradise life was still good. Adam and Eve lived in complete harmony and unity with God, just as a young child is connected to its mother.

Yet just as this connection with the mother is still unconscious in a newborn child, Adam and Eve also lived in unconscious oneness with God. It was only when their consciousness developed and they became aware of a sense of self, of their own identity, of the world around them and also of God, that they became separated from God and were driven from paradise. This 'expulsion' is described in the book of Genesis in a few brief images:

So he drove out man; and he placed Cherubim at the east of the Garden of Eden and a flaming sword which turned every way...[1]

In its apparent simplicity this story refers to the great spiritual destiny which mankind has experienced since descending to the earth, showing how we once lived in complete harmony with the divine world. When mankind started to feel 'at home' on earth and gradually became self-aware and conscious of the earth, this unity and harmony with the divine world gradually faded and man felt 'driven from paradise'.

In very simple terms one could also describe this process as follows: initially, mankind was still able to see clearly (though unconsciously) into higher worlds of light. This ability to see gradually diminished, until we were no longer able to perceive the angels clearly, or the radiant light from the divine world, or the absolute love which came to us from that world to embrace and sustain us. In the end, all that remained of this ancient ability to see were our dreams: the last vestiges of an ancient capacity for clairvoyance.

This process of descent to earth through evolution eventually closed the spiritual world to us entirely so that we could only perceive the things of the earth. The story of paradise from the Book of Genesis describes, in the most graphic terms, the sorrow, the impotence and the feeling of abandonment which mankind must have experienced in a previous age when the last vestiges of clairvoyance died in us.

It should be remembered, though, that what we are describing here in a few words is a process which took place over the course of millions of years. The essence of this process is this: while mankind still lived in the lap of the gods, or in and with God, we were utterly at one with the divine world, but this connection faded step by step, and was replaced by man's focus on the earth and, at the same time, his waking to consciousness and self-awareness. This was a process of awakening, separation and 'growing up'.

In both oriental and western esoteric traditions this great span of evolution is divided into four stages or 'cosmic seasons' sometimes known as the Golden, Silver, Copper and Iron eras.

Apart from Plato, who tells about this, there are also descriptions in, for example, the ancient Persian tradition: Mazdaism, in the Hindu tradition and in the Book of Daniel in the Bible. This shows that the insight into the course of these four cosmic seasons is part of the universal wisdom, the universal knowledge, from which all religions have grown.

These four cosmic seasons on the one hand reflect the descent of mankind from the spiritual world, his 'evolution' or 'development' and his removal from the spiritual world. On the other hand they refer to the 'involution' of man, his incorporation in the material world.

1. The first era, the Golden era, is also known as Krita Yuga or Satya Yuga. 'Krita' means perfect and 'satya' means golden.

    •   In this era mankind starts on his 'descent' to the earth. While he was still one with God, part of the being of God before this descent, man now descends to the earth as a divine spark to start on his journey through the material world, cloaked in a physical body: a journey that will require millions and millions of years and countless lives.

    •   During this era, man is still a companion of the spiritual world and at one with it. Although he is now physically on earth, spiritually he still resides mainly in the spiritual world.

    •   In fact, man still has the capacity to look into the higher worlds of light. You could say that the angels are still the playmates of man during this era.

    •   Knowledge and spiritual strength flowed directly from the spiritual world into mankind.

    •   While man could still clearly see into the different spiritual worlds, the physical reality on earth was perceived as a mist, hazily and not clearly defined. He was only 'awake' for a brief period of time. During this era, man 'slept' for most of the day, but this sleep was a state of clairvoyant (though unconscious) observation of the world of light.

    •   Death was during this time nothing other than the breaking of the connection with the physical body and the return to the spiritual world, the world of light, where man had spent so much time while he was asleep during his earthly life.

- Man was not yet able to stand on his own two legs, but was dependent on the angels, on the inflow and leadership of the spiritual world.

  We can also call this era the era of true religion. After all, religion means 'connection': the connection with the spiritual world. At that time there was no religion as we know it at present. Mankind *lived* in a connected way and therefore did not need a theory about this. Anyone who lives in a religious, 'connected' way does not need religion!

- Man was still wise, virtuous and loving and there was no place for evil on earth and in mankind.

- Man therefore did not yet cause any karma which had to be contemplated after death in kamaloka and worked out in a next life. Life in the Golden Era was truly imbued with peace and love on earth.

2. The second great evolutionary era is the Silver era, also known as Treta Yuga:[2]

   - During his period on earth, man was now not only given a physical body, but was also provided with an ethereal body. This acquisition of the ethereal body is described in the biblical story of Genesis. God created a figure of clay and breathed life into it:

     And the Lord God formed man of dust of the ground, and breathed into his nostrils the breath of life; and man became a living being.[3]

   - During the Golden era, man was able to look into the spiritual worlds of the angels and into the even higher regions of the archangels and the primeval forces. These three names, the angels, the archangels and the primeval forces, refer to three increasingly higher angelic spheres or beings of thought. During the Silver era, the world of the primeval forces closed to mankind and he was 'only' able to look into the sphere of the angels and archangels.

On the other hand something slowly became more clearly visible in the mist on earth: the animals started to light up for man.

We see that a transition takes place: in the spiritual world something closes, while on the other side, on earth, something becomes accessible, visible and can therefore be experienced. Slowly but steadily, man loses his connection with the spiritual world and step-by-step starts to feel at home on earth.

• The will impulses from the spiritual world become more blurred and reduce so that man has to learn to apply and use his own will. This development is accompanied by the first appearance of evil on the earth. Admittedly, man now disposes of his first own will impulses, but is still a long way from the awareness to use this will in accordance with the laws of cosmic love and cosmic will.

• This means that after his death, man is confronted for the first time with the consequences of his actions on earth: his karma. Furthermore, he cannot consciously ascend to the world of the primeval forces after his death because he has lost consciousness of this world and – because of his karma – the purity to ascend into this world.

• During the Silver era, man remembers the time before his birth when he was still at one with the divine world. What was still timeless in the Golden era, an eternal present, becomes a memory in the Silver era. This involves a loss, but also a gift, because memory is an essential condition for the development of the 'I', which starts in the next era.

3. The third great evolutionary era is the Copper era or Dvapara Yuga. Dvapara means: doubt. In this third era man increasingly loses awareness of his divine origin and his spiritual home, even though this world is not entirely closed and forgotten.

In this era man receives the astral body and gradually becomes at home in it. This enables him to feel even more at home in the material world. It also means that the divine centre of man is now cloaked in three different bodies and his great spiritual forces are less able to manifest and shine through these different cloaks.

The characteristics of this era are:

• The ancient clairvoyance becomes more and more blurred. Man is no longer able to see into the world of the archangels but only into the realm of the angels.

• On earth, the plant kingdom now starts to emerge from the mist, distinctly and clearly defined. Man's attention moves even further away from the spiritual world to the earth.

• Man now stands on the border of two worlds: the spiritual world and the world of matter on earth.

• There is an increase in evil. Wisdom, purity and the inner focus on the world of goodness are increasingly lost. The right inner attitude which is in accordance with divine and cosmic laws, becomes blurred and a selfish approach starts to take the place of the ancient wisdom.

• Karma, which accrues in man during his lifetime on earth, becomes weightier all the time. As a result, his period in the astral world after death gets longer. Man first has to gain insight into his past life and be purified in kamaloka. Moreover once he has passed through the astral world after death, he is not able to ascend further than the world of the angels. The higher spiritual worlds remain closed to him. He lacks the consciousness of these worlds and the purity and greatness of spirit to be able to enter these worlds and acquire new strengths from there.

4. The fourth great evolutionary era is the Iron era or Kali Yuga, the Dark Age. This is the darkest era on earth, in which the fall of man reaches the lowest point. During this era the 'I' awakens fully in man, first of all in its lowest, ego form. In general terms this era started in approximately 3000 BC. It is coming to an end in our time. We therefore also experience the start of another era that succeeds the Iron age.

    Characteristics of the Iron era:

    *   During this era the gates to the spiritual world are closed. Man is no longer able to see clearly into spirit realms, nor into the world of the angels. Man now knows – and above all, feels – that he has been driven from paradise. At the beginning of the Iron era only a few people were still able to ascend into the spiritual world along the path of initiation. However, at the start of our own time this possibility also came to an end.

    *   Man now feels fully at home on earth. He considers himself a man of the earth and forgets that he actually originates from the spiritual world and is, in his essence, a spiritual being. The mineral world on earth, the last world which had not been clearly visible to man, is now clearly defined and starts to form part of man's experience.

    *   At the same time there is a constant increase in evil. Now that man has forgotten the spiritual world and his spiritual origins, his own ego becomes the standard for his actions in the world. His own interests, his own thoughts and his own opinions take the place of the spiritual values

and the cosmic love which formed the basis for man's life in the past.

- In our own times, at the end of the Iron era, almost all the awareness of the spiritual world has been lost. More and more people think and believe that the visible world, the earth, is the only world that exists. For many this means that death is also the final end of life. The term 'God is dead!' was coined during the last century - and still sums up the experience of many today.

- Therefore we have actually become prisoners of the physical world, though it is because of this, cast back on ourselves, that the force of the 'I' awakens in us and we find in ourselves the strength to remain upright and survive in this world. In fact, mankind has now come to the verge of spiritual adulthood.

- The further man descended into the world of matter in the Iron era, the more difficult it becomes to enter the world of the angels after his death. He has lost his consciousness of that world, and in addition, the karma he has accumulated makes him so impure that this also prevents him from entering that world. This means that mankind becomes imprisoned in the astral world after his death. Many remain in this lower astral world between their lives on earth. Therefore the banishment from paradise now also takes place in the spiritual world after death. Man is expelled from paradise for a second time.

- The Iron era, and particularly the end of this era, is man's darkest hour. It is the period in which all the karma accumulated in previous eras is discharged and has to be processed and transformed. However, at the same time, it is also the great transition to a new Golden era, an era of peace and true love, which will one day, in the future, become reality again – though now in a conscious way.

- During our own time we are experiencing the great transition to the new era that succeeds the Iron era on earth. However, the night is darkest at the last hour before the first morning light breaks through. The last labour pains, the last contractions are the worst in giving birth. This age in which we live is a time of transition: on the one hand, a time of expectation, on the other hand, a time of increasing difficulties, war, violence, crime and also natural disasters.

As towards the end of the Iron era, more and more people became 'stuck' in the astral world after their death and were unable to 'ascend' to higher spiritual worlds, something occurred that reopened the passage from the astral world to the higher worlds of light again. This event – to which the next chapter will be devoted – is of unimaginable importance for all life on earth.

For when human spirits started to be able to ascend to the light worlds again, they could take from these higher worlds new spiritual forces with them to their next life on earth. These contribute to the possibility of a transformation from the darkest depths of the Iron era to the new Golden era we have mentioned. In the spiritual world something happens, which then takes effect for life on earth.

This revolution which opened the gateway to higher spiritual worlds was achieved by Jesus who became the Christ.

Notes

1   Genesis 3:24
2   In the oriental tradition the second great era is not always known as the Silver era but sometimes as the Copper era. The subsequent era which – based on the book of Daniel in the Bible, is called the Copper era in the western tradition, is called the Silver era in eastern teachings.
3   Genesis 2:7

11. *The Revolution and Renewal Performed by Christ*

Life after death before the coming of Christ

It is not only the New Testament and many ancient legends, but also a number of apocryphal Gospels which describe how Jesus Christ entered the realm of death after his death on the cross of Golgotha, awakening and liberating the dead there.

The apocryphal Gospel of Nicodemus mentions one of these accounts. It describes the following event, which took place in the night of Good Friday to Easter Saturday in the underworld, as the realm of the dead is sometimes called:

> Thus we were in the underworld with all of those who had been asleep there from the beginning, but in the midnight hour a light entered the darkness as though it were the sun, and it shone and we were all lit up and saw each other. [1]

The condition in which the dead remained before Jesus Christ entered the realm of the dead, i.e., the lower astral world, was one of indistinct darkness. This is because people's souls were so dimmed as a result of developments described in the last chapter that the light of the divine world could no longer reach them. The dead could not see each other either. In the realm of death there was an atmosphere of dark, miserable loneliness, where the dead led a life with no prospects at all. It was this sense of the life after death as a dark underworld that gave rise to the proverb coined in Greek and Roman times that 'It is better to be a beggar in this world than a king in the realm of the shades.'

That is how dire the conditions were after death in the centuries before Christ came to the earth.

Because of the shadowy darkness in which the dead resided, they were not only unable to reach each other, but it had also become impossible for them to maintain contact with people alive on earth.

During the Iron era, therefore, mankind's evolution on earth had almost come to a standstill. After death, the dead could no longer ascend to the higher worlds of light, and could therefore not acquire new strength or inspiration for their next life on earth. Stagnation occurred and mankind was on an increasingly downward path, physically, soulwise, and spiritually. Furthermore, because of deeper incarnation in the material world, people increasingly fell under the influence of the forces of darkness. Their souls were increasingly in danger of coming under the power of demons, because they were becoming emptier and less spiritual all the time. Such demons had different intentions for mankind than the divine forces.[2]

As a result of all these negative conditions, human bodies became so weak that in the fairly close future people would no longer have been able to reincarnate on earth, nor, therefore, evolve any further.[3] It was clear that if nothing happened, the end of mankind was nigh.

Christ's advent on earth and its consequences

It was in those days of deep darkness when the future and evolution of mankind were at stake that the greatest event of all time took place. The spirit of Christ descended from the greatest heights of the divine world to the earth and came to dwell in Jesus of Nazareth. This happened at the baptism in the river Jordan. Jesus of Nazareth therefore became Jesus Christ.[4]

Three years later, Christ was crucified and died on Golgotha. But in the following days He vanquished death and appeared to His disciples in a new body. With this act, the spirit of Christ opened up the path to the divine worlds of light for man once again. How did this happen?

When he was crucified, the blood of Jesus Christ flowed from his wounds into the earth. This blood however was not ordinary blood. It was blood that was worked through by the spirit of Christ in the three years that he had lived on earth since the baptism in the river Jordan. In these three years the Christ being had fully transformed the blood of Jesus Christ into his own divine substance.

So when this blood flowed into the earth on Golgotha, with it came the divine and renewing strength of the Christ being himself. This now flowed from Golgotha into the whole of creation. From that moment on, the whole of the physical world of matter, the ethereal, the astral and the higher spiritual worlds were permeated with his divine substance and energy. And so were the physical, ethereal, and astral bodies of all human beings, plants, animals, and the earth itself.

This was the first part of the new connection that the Christ being made with the Creation.

The second part took place at Whitsuntide, when the disciples were together in Jerusalem. When the wind and the flames appeared over the heads of those who were gathered, the spirit of Christ, the Holy Spirit, descended into the hearts, souls and spiritual core of those who were present - and with them into the whole of mankind.

From that moment on the spirit of Christ lived in the heart and the 'I' of each human being on earth.

This event brought an enormous change in us human beings. For with this deed the Christ being created a new connection between our ordinary self or ego and our spiritual self, the divine core in our hearts. This new connection between the ego and the spirit self enabled us to become inwardly active ourselves and to start an inner, personal spiritual process which eventually will lead us back to the higher worlds of light.

Through his deed on Golgotha and at Whitsuntide the renewing and strengthening forces of Christ reconnected the whole of creation with the divine world. By doing so, Christ not only conquered death and prevented the destruction of mankind in the world of matter, but he also reopened the gates to the higher spiritual worlds again, for our life on earth and for our life after death.

Christ proved to be stronger than the forces of darkness, and also stronger than the forces of death. This is also shown by the fact that after His death Christ did not remain imprisoned in the realm of death, the lower astral world, as the great majority of people had done before Him. On the contrary, instead of being overwhelmed by darkness, he brought light and consciousness to the darkness and awakened the dead who were already there, liberating them from their imprisonment.

The Gospel of Nicodemus graphically describes how Jesus Christ, the King of Worship as he is known in that gospel, went to work in the realm of death. When He arrives in the underworld after His death, the angels who accompany Christ command both Satan, the Prince of Darkness, and the Prince of the Underworld (Death) to open the gates so that the divine light, the King of Worship can enter. The Prince of Darkness and the Prince of the Underworld do not want to do this because they know that their power will be undermined. Instead of opening the gates, they bar them even more firmly. Subsequently, the gospel describes how the angels of the Lord destroy the copper gates and smash the iron bars. The Gospel of Nicodemus continues:

> And the King of Worship entered in the form of a man and the whole of the darkness of hell was filled with a light.

The King of Worship then seizes the Prince of Princes, Satan, delivers him to the angels, and says:

> Shackle him with iron shackles, hand and feet, neck and mouth.

Then he is handed to the Prince of the Underworld with the words:

> Take him and keep him safe until my second coming.

Subsequently the King of Worship awakens the dead who are present and calls upon them to go with him, taking them with him to paradise.

Like all the other gospels, the Gospel of Nicodemus not only describes a spiritual reality, but also tells those who have 'ears to hear' other hidden truths in a mystery language. One of these truths is that, through His coming and His work in the realm of death, the spirit of Christ reversed the separation from the divine world. Shattering the *copper gates* and smashing the *iron* bolts means that at that moment Christ reopened the gates to the higher regions of the spiritual worlds which had been closed to mankind during the Copper and Iron eras. The souls of the dead can now follow Him to paradise, bathed in His light, i.e. they go to the higher worlds of light and can therefore evolve further.

The light which the spirit of Christ shines into the darkness of the realm of death means that the dead are once again able to see and experience each other. This is clear from the text quoted above: '…in the midnight hour, a light entered this darkness like a sun and it shone and we were lit up and *we saw each other*.' The light of Christ linked and united mankind in a new way. After the events on Golgotha this applies wherever He is present and works: both amongst the dead in the spiritual world, between people on earth, and between those who remain behind on earth and those who have passed through the gates of death.

The work of Jesus Christ in the life after death

One of the questions which often arises is: Will I meet Jesus Christ in my life after death? Is anything known about this and can anything be said?

Rudolf Steiner in particular had a great deal to say about this. He revealed – in many different ways and from many different perspectives – that in life after death Jesus Christ accompanies and helps us through the different regions to the higher worlds of light. In the warm mantle of the light of His love, we look back at the earthly life we have just finished.

As we saw before, people who have had a near-death experience talk about a being of light radiating love. Who is this being of light? An angel? An even higher spiritual being? Jesus Christ himself?

In the time before Christ descended to earth, the dead did not go any further than the 'underworld', the lower regions of the astral world. We saw that this world was 'hazy, shadowy and dark', and therefore also known as 'Hell'. The spiritual beings of light were unable to reach the dead and were therefore unable to give them new strength. Consequently the consciousness of the dead was not only dulled but also, as we saw, caught up in increasing decline. It was merely a matter of time before souls would lose all consciousness when they entered death.

This would have meant that we lost not only our connection with the spiritual world, but also our immortality. After all, immortality means that our consciousness continues to exist after death.

However, since Golgotha, the spirit of Christ lives in us. He carries us when we die. And it is through him that our *consciousness is restored to us in the spiritual world after death.*[5] This does not always happen immediately after death for everyone, but after a longer or shorter period of dwelling in darkness or shadows, consciousness lights up again. Thanks to the working of Christ in us, this new consciousness can develop ever further in the life after death. It can even grow to the highest worlds of light. In fact there are no limits to the growth of our consciousness. Our spirit is of divine origin: if this develops in us, higher and higher regions will open up to us forever. That is what is meant by immortality.

After death, we not only gain new consciousness, but also self-awareness. It appears that the effect of the spirit of Christ during our lifetime means that we are able to retain our individual, personal consciousness after death. At the same time we experience that we are at one with each other there, in contrast with our life on earth.

After our death we also gain an insight into ourselves, into other people and into the events which we experienced during our lifetime and the relationship we had with everything. The fact that we look back at our lives and can learn from them, both in the ethereal world just after death and in the astral world, is also due to the working of Christ in us. We can look back at our life in an atmosphere of love and light, experience it again, and gain insight and understanding so that we can eventually draw up the balance of what was good and what needs to be resolved and changed.

Through the spirit of Christ we also gain a better insight into the meaning of life on earth, the relationship between the divine world and mankind, the laws of the universe and the goal towards which mankind is travelling.

The being of light and Jesus Christ

In previous chapters we have seen that many people who have a near-death experience meet a being who emits an incredibly intense and radiant light.

It is fascinating to find that the being of light which people refer to when they have a near-death experience has all sorts of characteristics which Jesus Christ also has. Before we go into this in more detail, we would like to make a number of other comments.

Researchers who have studied the experiences of people who were clinically dead and spent some time on the other side have come to the conclusion that after death people pass through a number of stages. These stages reveal a path or journey. Researchers emphasise that each near-death experience is different from every other, yet they all contain some common features. The path starts with separation from the physical body and consists of the following stages:

1. The person rises up from her body.
2. She finds herself in a dark void.
3. She floats through a tunnel at great speed.
4. She sees and communicates with relatives and acquaintances who have died (a stage which can occur at different moments).
5. She moves towards a bright light which becomes larger until she is consumed by it.
6. She meets a being of light with a tremendous, total love and absolute knowledge.
7. The light asks her what she has done with her life.
8. The person looks back at her life; certain events from her life

are evoked and she experiences the effects which her acts had on other people.

9. She is taken up by and has a sense of absolute love and knowledge.

10. She passes through the light and sees crystals or dizzyingly magnificent cities where people live.

11. She then has a choice of whether or not to return, and the light emphasises that she has not yet completed her task on earth, or that her loved ones still miss her.

12. She returns and experiences the same stages in reverse order and at an accelerated rate, and suddenly finds that she is back in her physical body.[6]

Let us look again at a number of near-death experiences, relating them to these first ten stages.

A middle-aged woman, Elaine Winner, 'died' as a result of a number of successive strokes and had a near-death experience. Shortly before, she had been given the last rites by a priest in her room in the intensive care department in the hospital. She recounted how she felt herself being lifted up from her body as she died and entered a dark void. Soon afterwards she felt that she was moving through a long tunnel and a gradually increasing light approached at the end of the tunnel. Elaine Winner recounted:

It is not the same sort of light that we have here. It is brighter. It was a very comforting light and I felt that I was moving towards it. I was not conscious of a physical body and I floated towards it at an incredible speed. I had the feeling: through Me you will have eternal life.[7]

What was happening here? Like most other people who have had a near-death experience she first found herself in the dark just after she died. She passed through a dark void and a dark tunnel, and only then met the light. This reveals that during or after death we pass through regions in the spiritual world which are dark.

After death we appear to be aware of what is happening very quickly. If this were not the case, people who have near-death experiences would not be able to remember anything. Others have said that just after death everything became 'hazy'. In this hazy state, the dead are attracted by a source of light. Some say that the 'mist' is suddenly lit up by a source of light. At the same time, it is also a point of orientation. All the people who have had a near-death experience and encountered this being of light have gone towards it.

When we look at this experience in relation to what we discussed above about the effects which Jesus Christ had on life after death, we see that these correspond in a general way. The darkness or shadows which occur after death are lit up and are driven out by the source of light.

Before those who 'died' arrive at the light, they have usually realised that they have died. At the same time, they become aware that they continue to exist. Elaine Winner continued:

> In those few fractions of a second I realised that there is no such thing as death. The death we see is the death of the physical body. Your inner core, the spirit or the soul never dies, but lives on.

Isn't it striking how strong her consciousness is just after death? It is at a much higher level than it was during her daily life on earth. Elaine not only soon realised that she had died, but at the same time also gained a comprehensive insight into the essence of death: she became aware that death only affects the physical body and that the inner core, the spirit or soul never dies, but lives on forever.

Elaine Winner then approached the source of light:

> When I went closer to the light I felt the unimaginable love
> which the light radiated. I felt understanding, I felt
> forgiveness and I felt many other things at the same time. You
> cannot even compare this love (of the light) to the love of the
> one person who loves you more than anyone in the world.
> The love was so total, so absolute that I could not imagine it.

George Ritchie, whose journey through the spiritual world was
described in chapter 3, says that he realised that this man of light
was Jesus, the Son of God. But it appeared to be a very different
Jesus from the one he had known from Sunday school. The figure
standing in front of him was a pillar of strength, older than time
itself, and yet more modern than anyone he had ever met. Ritchie
noted that the being of light radiated an intense love and that it
was familiar with all his acts and thoughts:

> Far more even than power, what emanated from this Presence
> was unconditional love. An astonishing love. A love beyond
> my wildest imagining. This love knew every unlovable thing
> about me – the quarrels with my step-mother, my explosive
> temper, the sex thoughts I could never control, every mean,
> selfish thought and action since the day I was born – and
> accepted and loved me just the same.

At the moment that this man of light entered his hospital room,
Ritchie's whole life appeared before him:

> When I say He knew everything about me, this was simply an
> observable fact. For into the room along with His radiant
> presence – simultaneously, though in telling about it I have to
> describe them one by one – had also entered every single

episode of my entire life. Everything that had ever happened to me was simply there, in full view, contemporary and current…

Ritchie noted that all these comprehensive, detailed and exact images of memory were radiated by this being of light. It was as though they came forth from his inner being. The images of his life started when this figure of light entered his hospital room. It appeared to be familiar with all the thoughts and deeds which Ritchie had experienced through the twenty years of his life.

While he looked at these images, Ritchie was confronted with an inner question: *What have you done with your life?* In other words, what have you achieved in the valuable time you were allotted? What have you done which has had permanent value? Ritchie felt that he was not asked this in order to pressurise him, but so that he would become aware of the value of his life. A woman who met the being of light said that she was asked about her own contribution to mankind, without any words, but by means of a direct exchange of thoughts. She too was confronted with a question which made her more aware.

Ritchie answered the question posed by the light by recounting everything he had achieved during his lifetime. But when he looked back he saw that he had always been concerned with and worried about *himself* in a short-sighted and insistent way. The being of light widened his focus and suddenly made him aware what really matters in life:

> He wasn't asking about accomplishments and awards. The question, like everything else proceeding from Him, had to do with love. How much have you loved with your life. Have you loved others as I am loving you? Totally? Unconditionally?

Others also start to realise what life is about when they look back together with the being of light. One woman gave the following account:

> I realised that everyone is sent to the earth to do and learn certain things. For example, to be loving to other people, to discover that human relationships and love are the most important thing of all and not materialistic things. To realise that everything you do in life is recorded and has an effect, even if you do not pay any attention to this at the moment itself.[8]

She gives an example of the following situation: you are in a hurry and have to wait at traffic lights. The person in the car in front of you does not see that the light has turned green because she is not taking any notice. What do you do in this situation? Do you get angry and start to sound the horn or do you have understanding and patience?

What conclusions can we draw from all this?

- It is clear that the being of light spreads consciousness and love wherever it appears.
- The survey of our life and the being of light are interrelated. The images of our past life emerge from the inner core of that being.
- The being of light awakens the consciousness of anyone he meets. This inner awakening occurs in a free and unforced way. He asks questions. These questions show that life on earth is not meaningless, but has a purpose. 'What did you do with the time you were allotted? What did you make of it? What was your contribution to the development of mankind?' These questions help us to wake up inwardly.
- The being of light makes us aware of cosmic love as the very fabric of life.

According to Kenneth Ring, a researcher into near-death experiences, these universal values are *remembered* in a vivid and powerful way. You have an insight into your life, you remember these essential values and recognise them, and all this together means that you want to change your life in accordance with these values. Every person who has had a near-death experience is, he says, reminded of these universal values.

It is striking, though, that every person who has looked back at her own life in this way says that the being of light never passes judgemental comments, but always embraces her with his warm love, showing all sorts of things to help us learn from them. One person stressed:

> ... not what I *should* have done, because this would have been moralising, but what I *could* have done – an open invitation which left me entirely free to follow his suggestions or to cast them aside.[9]

Again we see the respectful way in which the being of light deals with and relates to people, leaving them free to make their own decisions. This understanding, love and respect does not mean that looking back in this way is not a confrontational experience – it still causes pain. This applies particularly when you become aware of what you have done to other people. One man with a criminal past who relived his whole criminal career, including all the minor injuries which he had inflicted on others quite unconsciously, by his thoughtless words, looks and omissions, related:

> Nothing was left out of this nightmare of pain I had caused, but the worst was that every pain I had done to others I could now feel myself.[10]

It appears that the dead are able to tolerate this painful confrontation with themselves only because the being of light stands next to them and supports them with his all-embracing love. For some people, looking back at their past life is so shocking that they are in danger of being overwhelmed by it. But the embracing love of the being of light gives them the inner courage and the strength to be able to deal with it. One man recounted:

> The overriding feeling I had looking back over my life was that it would have been emotionally destructive if I had not felt the love of my friend (the being of light) and his friends while I looked at these things. I was able to feel this love. Every time that I became upset, they stopped the images for a while and comforted me.[11]

Is this being of light the Christ?

Everyone who has had a near-death experience and has met this being of light is confronted with questions. For some people it is immediately obvious that it is Jesus, the Son of God. For others it is Christ or God or an angel. There are also people who simply do not know and just call him the 'being of light'.

Let us take a look at the different characteristics and actions of the being of light and see how these compare with the essence of Jesus Christ.

One of the first elements we come across is that the being of light drives out the darkness which engulfs those who die just after death. It brings light, consciousness and love. It appears to be the central point to which everyone is attracted and towards which everyone wants to move. In addition, the being of light evokes the conscious self-awareness of everyone he meets by means of questions. All the images of the past life appear to come from his inner core. He is familiar with everything that has happened and with every thought and deed of those concerned. He indicates how they could have related to other people with more understanding and love.

His comprehensive understanding for those who are looking back at their life and his supportive and strengthening love is another important element. So is his respect for the dead as people struggling to become who they are, and leaving them free in their process. Many people state that in his presence, they felt that they were forgiven for what they had done wrong.

Does all this together not clearly indicate that the being of light is related to Jesus Christ and that the spirit of Christ is working in him?

One of the people who had a near-death experience, Thomas Benedict Mellen, asked the being of light who he was. Mellen told Kenneth Ring that his question was answered as follows:

> Then the Light revealed itself to me and lifted me up to a level I had not been to before. It was not a verbal explanation; it was more like telepathic communication, very vivid. I could feel it, I could feel the light. The light responded and manifested itself at a different level. And the message was: 'Yes, for most people, depending on their background, I am Jesus, Buddha, Krishna…

The being was silent after these words. Mellen then asked: 'But who are you *really*?' Mellen describes what happened next:

> Then the Light changed into what I can only call a pattern, a mandala of souls of people and I saw that what we call the 'higher self' in each of us is actually a sort of matrix. It is also a channel connecting us to the source; every one of us is directly descended from this source, without any intermediaries. It was completely clear to me that all these

higher selves were collected in one being, all people together form one being. We are actually the same being or different aspects of the same being.[12]

This description is reminiscent of the scene of Pentecost: the spirit of Christ which lives in each individual person in an individual way and also connects and links people together at the same time. At the beginning of the last century, Rudolf Steiner said: 'Since Golgotha, the spirit of Christ has appeared as the true self of each individual person and at the same time as the higher self of all humanity.'[13]

Notes

1   *The Gospel According to Nicodemus*
2   It would go beyond the scope of this book to describe evil or adversary forces in detail. Steiner speaks at length about the enemies of human evolution, Lucifer, Ahriman and the Asuras, who try in varying ways to 'tempt' the human being and divert him from a true evolutionary path. For more on this see *Evil*, Rudolf Steiner Press 1997; and many other texts by Steiner (see Bibliography)
3   We saw before that we need earthly conditions to evolve, for against the resistance these conditions offer we can exercise our capacities and develop them.
4   See Rudolf Steiner: *Esoteric Christianity*
5   Rudolf Steiner, *Aus den Inhalten der esoterischen Stunden* III lecture, 6 January 1913
6   Based on: Charles P. Flynn: *After the Beyond: Human Transformation and the Near-Death Experience*
7   Ibid
8   Kenneth Ring/Evelyn Elsaesser Valarino: *Lessons From the Light: What We Can Learn from the Near-Death Experience*
9   Ibid
10   Ibid
11   Ibid
12   Ibid
13   Rudolf Steiner: *The Gospel of St John*, Rudolf Steiner Press, London, 1988

12. The Connection Between the Dead and the Living

When we die we separate from the physical body. This separation occurs during a 'sleeping state', i.e., unconsciously. Thanks to the working of Christ in us we gradually wake up in the spiritual world and a whole new world opens up to us. If we have been engaged in spiritual or religious matters during our time on earth, we will understand where we are more quickly than if we have not done so. In fact there are also those who do not wish to awaken. On earth they did not believe in life after death, and initially they also refused to recognise this in the spiritual world.

Waking up in the spiritual world brings a deep feeling of joy and satisfaction at the atmosphere which prevails there, and feelings of relief at no longer having a physical body. This is followed, as we saw, by looking back at the life which has been led.

Yet as we look back we also start to miss and long for the loved ones who have remained behind on earth. The dead naturally miss the physical closeness and contact with those they have left behind.

Admittedly they now live in the spiritual world, but they are still wholly connected to life on earth and with those they have left behind, with their entire being. The dead also feel the pain which their departure has caused others. The heightened consciousness in which they live now shows that essentially there is absolutely no separation between the dead and the living and that the ties of love which developed on earth *never cease to exist.* The dead constantly try to reveal this to the living in all sorts of ways. Those who remain behind on earth do not usually have this knowledge and insight and it is therefore very different for them. At most, they sometimes *feel* that their loved ones who have died are nearby, without being able to give this feeling a place in their views on life after death. For example, the pastor Ter Linden whom we quoted in chapter 1 talked about the situation after his wife's death:

> It is true that there is a painful silence now, but at the same time it is a silence full of her presence.[1]

How can it be that the dead are able to feel what happens in the souls of those who remain behind? This is because – no matter how unbelievable this may sound to us here on earth – they live *in* and *around* us. The world of the spheres to which the dead go, whether we call it the hereafter, heaven or the spiritual world, is not separated from us, but wholly permeates our life on earth. As earthly people we form part of the ethereal world with our ethereal body. With our astral body we live in the astral world or world of the soul. And with our spirit self, our divine centre, we are part of the higher spiritual worlds of light. The living and the dead are *only separated from each other at the physical level.*

What does all this mean for contact with the dead? It means that in my ethereal body I live in the *same* ethereal world as the dead who have been looking back at their lives after they have died. With my soul or astral body I live in the *same* astral world as the dead who look back for the second time and assimilate their experiences on earth. With my spiritual self, my divine core, I live in the same spiritual world of light, the heavenly world or devachan, as that where the dead go after death.

The difference between those who have died and those who remain behind on earth is that the latter remain closed off in their physical bodies on earth from this ethereal, spiritual and astral world. Of course, this is not the whole reality, but an illusion which our earthly intellect presents to us. We come closest to the truth when we say that the spiritual worlds are largely unconscious for people on earth. This is also expressed in the fact that of all the memories which have been stored during life on earth and which are collected in the ethereal body, only a relatively small proportion are consciously remembered. The remainder are unconscious. The content of the largest part of our ethereal body is therefore unconscious for us. The same applies to all the emotions, thoughts, intentions, ideals, efforts and so on, which have occurred throughout life up to now and which reside in our astral body. We only partly remember these. That is due to our earthly consciousness, our intellect.

The sense that we are separated from the dead, therefore, as people living on earth, is merely a matter of our earthly consciousness.

When we are asleep at night, we are not conscious of all the things in our bedroom: the chair, the table, clothes, all sorts of bits and pieces. Just as we do not observe these physical articles around us when we are asleep, we do not see those with whom we live together in the ethereal, astral and higher spiritual world when we are awake.

On the other hand, if we were to suddenly wake up spiritually in these other regions and become aware of the ethereal, astral and higher world of light, we would immediately encounter and recognise all our loved ones and friends who are on the other side. For many who have lost a dear one to death, this idea is too wonderful to even think about.

Yet these sorts of meetings between the living and the dead *do take place*, although we are not conscious of this! At night, when we fall asleep, our astral body and our divine centre separate from our physical and ethereal body, as we saw in chapter 5. With our astral body and our spirit, we then rise up to the astral and spiritual world of light, the worlds where the dead reside. In this way we come face to face with our loved ones who have died, unhindered by our physical, earthly consciousness. We can 'speak' to each other there and remain in each other's company until it is time to wake.

Those who live on earth and those who live in the spiritual world after death therefore reach each other through the realms which they have in common. This means that the dead not only perceive and experience all the feelings, thoughts, emotions, impulses in our soul and spirit, but also the more spiritual elements, such as ideals, higher intentions, spiritual insights and forces of love. The dead no longer have a physical body and are therefore not restricted by it. They perceive our body as a vague mist, but can see the movements of our inner being outlined extremely clearly.

The thoughts and feelings of those who remain behind on earth, which are sent to the dead, are therefore experienced immediately. Warm, loving feelings and thoughts are a great gift for the dead. They assimilate them and feel inner warmth and happiness as a result. Good, warm thoughts always reach the dead, wherever they are. In turn, the connections which are formed in this way give the dead the opportunity to send those who have remained behind their love, warmth and inspirations. In this way it is possible for both to feel connected to each other, to console and encourage each other. This strengthens their relationship.

Obviously it is not only positive feelings and thoughts which those who have died perceive. Feelings of anger and hatred also enter them directly, causing them suffering. Such negative thoughts and feelings also connect the dead to the earth and to those who are sending them – which shows how important it is for both parties to pass through processes of assimilation to eventually arrive at forgiveness. It is only when this has been achieved that the relationship can be resolved and renewed so that it can develop further.

Conditions for contact

As long as the dead remain in the astral world or the world of the soul, they can only contact the living if the latter make this possible with their spirit and soul, i.e., their thoughts and feelings. This is, amongst other things, because the dead are entirely taken up in the world of the soul by assimilating the life they have lived. It is only when they have reached the higher world of light that the dead can form their own connections with the living and become active in them.[2]

This means that people living on earth must create the conditions for contact to be possible. If they no longer think of the dead, because they assume that everything ends with death and therefore their loved ones no longer exist, the dead cannot reach those who have been left behind. The same applies if the living are entirely taken up by their own grief and do not send any free and loving thoughts to the other person. Nor can connection be established if the person who has been left behind is completely taken up by earthly and material things and does not have any spiritual thoughts or feelings. The dead can only make contact with an element in the human soul that is spiritual and unselfish. This applies increasingly as the individual on the other side develops spiritually and becomes more liberated from the earth.

Rudolf Steiner recounted that visionaries experience shocking things in this respect in the regions where the dead reside.[3] For example, he often came across people in the spiritual world who had died and led an extremely lonely existence. They had not developed spiritually on earth and therefore lacked the 'light' that could help them to learn to see and understand the spiritual world around them. In addition, they were unable to make contact with the loved ones they had left behind on earth because these people did not have any spiritual thoughts either. Steiner mentioned the example of a man who had died and left his wife behind on earth. During his lifetime he had come back home from his work happy every day. After a tiring day his life with his wife made everything right for him. He had loved his wife with all his heart. Even now, all his thoughts and memories were focused on her and he missed her. He told Rudolf Steiner that he was constantly focusing on the earth, but could not find his wife. Because of what he had learned in the spiritual world, he now knew that she must be there somewhere, but it was just as though she had dissolved. He was very sad about this and felt very lonely.

When Steiner studied this problem he realised that this was because the man's wife did not have any spiritual thoughts or ideas and was totally absorbed in appearances, because of the materialistic culture in which she had grown up. As a result she was not visible in the spiritual world where her husband resided and so he was unable to contact her, and could therefore not be part of her life. Rudolf Steiner added that the dead can have the feeling, like this man, that they are held back or imprisoned and therefore cannot penetrate to those with whom they were deeply connected on earth. The cause of this sad situation lies primarily in those who remain behind on earth.

For the dead, contact with those with whom they were connected on earth is very important for a number of reasons. Anyone who dies and enters the spiritual world must get used to this new environment. In a sense, the transition to this world is comparable to moving to a foreign country. You are not yet familiar with the language or the customs and you first have to get used to many of the things you encounter. It is only gradually that you start to feel at home.

Admittedly, after death you are surrounded by spiritual beings of light, by angels and other 'dead' individuals in an atmosphere of caring love, but you do not immediately have the ability to make contact with them. This only becomes possible once you have gained spiritual liberation by working through your past life, so that you can kindle the inner light enabling you to approach the spiritual beings around you.

Therefore, on the one hand, we feel the atmosphere of truth and goodness which prevails in the spiritual world when we arrive; but on the other hand, we miss those we have left behind and feel lonely. In this situation it is obviously a great consolation to be able to contact the members of our family or friends who are still alive on earth, and feel connected to them. If we are not able to do this because they do not think about us or do not have any spiritual thoughts, our loneliness in the spiritual world increases. In our time, when materialistic thoughts have become paramount, many people think that there is no life after death. The result is that many of the dead will not be able to contact their partners, family members or friends. This not only results in spiritual loneliness on both sides, but also hinders the help, inspiration and encouragement which the dead can in their turn give from the spiritual world.

The significance of people on earth for the dead

There is another reason why the interaction between the dead on the one hand, and those who have been left behind on the other hand, is so important. This is because the dead *need spiritual knowledge which can only be acquired on earth*, for the assimilation of their past lives and for their continued journey through the spiritual world. Above all they need this for the work which they will carry out in future from the higher world of light. Mysteriously, spiritual beings, including the dead, are able to view some things in the spiritual world, but cannot always understand or use them very easily. They can only do this with the help of spiritual knowledge and spiritual insight which have been acquired by human beings on earth.[4]

When we read an inspiring book such as the Bible, and do so not only with our intellect but also with our feelings – so that we have an inner experience of what we read – this insight lights up in the spiritual worlds. Through our thoughts and feelings the dead and other spiritual beings can then acquire the knowledge which they need for their continued spiritual work, both in the cosmos and on earth. In this way we see how people on earth and beings in the spiritual world depend on each other for their mutual development and for the continued development of mankind. This shows the importance of the earth for this whole development. It was certainly not created without reason.

It is astonishing to realise that the dead need *us* here on earth to understand certain things and to assimilate them as insights. Perhaps this becomes more understandable when we realise that the true insights that we achieve here on earth pass through *four* worlds: the physical world, the ethereal world, the astral world or world of the soul, and the spiritual world of light. These are worlds in which *the spirit of Christ lives and works* since the events on Golgotha.

Because of this, because the spirit of Christ is at work in these four worlds, true insights on earth are transformed into something which cannot be found in such a form in the spiritual world. This means that the world on earth *adds* something to these insights that enhances and enriches life in the spiritual world. This great secret relates to the descent of the spirit of Christ to life on earth.

Rudolf Steiner repeatedly pointed out how the dead long for spiritual nourishment which can only be granted them by the living: spiritual knowledge and insight which have passed through the soul and spirit of human beings on earth.

But the longing which the dead have for such earth-imbued spiritual nourishment, which only those who have remained on earth can give them, is something they are often unable to obtain from them. Rudolf Steiner observed how, when the astral body and 'I' of living people ascend during sleep, the dead approach their loved ones, longingly waiting to see whether they have brought them any spiritual nourishment which they can use. Steiner saw how disappointed they were when it became apparent that these people might not have had a single religious feeling or spiritual thought, or experienced anything in their soul in the previous day which the dead can absorb. In this case the dead suffer 'spiritual hunger'. Steiner talks about the almost epidemic 'spiritual starvation' which can be found amongst the dead in the spiritual world as a result of the increasing materialism on earth. In particular, he saw people who had not been at all concerned with spiritual wisdom on earth yearning for this nourishment.

Subsequently he urged people to read books or other texts containing spiritual or religious insights for the dead. Many people have listened to his advice and have made it a habit to think about the dead and regularly read inspirational books or poems to them. Some of them have told us that they felt that it was not only the dead whom they knew who came to listen, but that others also drew near to listen, even though these were not personally known to them.

In fact clairvoyants often experience this during lectures on spiritual subjects: spiritual beings such as angels and the dead listen along with the earthly people who are attending. When Rittelmeyer asked whether Steiner had ever met his (Rittelmeyer's) dead mother in the spiritual world, Rudolf Steiner answered: 'When you come to listen to a lecture there is often a presence there whom I believe to be your mother. She brings a

A CHRISTIAN BOOK OF THE DEAD

few others with her. She is rather restless and walks about a bit. But she takes an active part in your spiritual life.'[5]

What does this mean for us living on earth? Perhaps when we read something before we go to sleep at night to people who have died, and with whom we had a relationship, we help them enormously in their development. We not only help them, but also other dead people who come with them, who also long for these insights. By doing this we contribute to building a bridge between the living and the dead. This bridge makes it possible for them in turn to inspire, encourage, and help those who live on earth.

The essence of the contact

This raises the question of what is the essence of the contact between the living on earth, and the dead in the spiritual world. The answer is that when the living and the dead interact and develop spiritual strengths and insights together, they enable high spiritual beings to further human development on earth. Yet in order to achieve this ambitious goal, both sides must be inwardly prepared to grow spiritually, personally and in relation to each other. If we consciously work on this, the power of the spirit of Christ can become active in us and between us. The Gospel according to St. Matthew describes this in the following words: 'Where there are two or more united in my name, I am among them.'[6]

Because of the sacrifice made by Christ, which means that the spirit of Christ is always in us and with us, both in life on earth and in life after death, the living and the dead can reach each other and continue along a spiritual path together. If we create the right conditions, truly communicate with each other, and assimilate our relationship on earth, the spirit of Christ can give us new insights, renew us and establish a new kind of contact between us.

114

We have said that the contact between the living and the dead is only possible when those who remain behind are conscious that the other person is still there, and that this relationship goes on after death. In order to achieve this, the dead do everything they can to show themselves to the living. They do so in the hope that this approach will lead to inner communication between them and those who have been left behind. Many people who have lost loved ones feel their presence around them. As the pastor Ter Linden said, they experience the fullness of this presence in the painful silence which follows after their departure.

In some cases those who have died will show themselves to their loved ones on earth just after their death. It is as though they want to say: Remember, I am still here. Because they are still so close to the physical world on earth, they are able to make themselves visible for a short moment in their ethereal body. A woman, whose mother-in-law had died of cancer, told the following story:

In the night after his mother's funeral, my husband Ben and I went home where the members of his family were present. We arrived quite late. When we got back in the car after the visit, I looked through the front door and saw his mother standing there in the opening of the door. She waved to us! She looked as she always did – it was certainly her. She looked very calm, very healthy, and younger. In the past she always used to say goodbye at the door when we had visited. This time it was exactly as it had been many times before.

I looked at Ben and said: 'Did you see…?' and then he started to cry. I realised that we had both seen his mother at the same time, but Ben was not able to talk about it. When I had looked at him, she disappeared. I think I saw his mother to confirm Ben's experience, so that he would know that it had not been a product of his imagination.[7]

In the following example, the dead father was not visible, but was present in a very tangible way. He clearly came to say goodbye to his daughter, but also to share an intense spiritual experience with her. The daughter related:

> My father had lung cancer. A technically successful operation was followed by one complication after another. There were many harrowing weeks in which hope and fear alternated. My brothers and I wanted to keep him with us so much, and he wanted to live as well. He had so many plans. He was also afraid of death, but unfortunately did not want to talk about it. Once he was in intensive care after the operation, connected to all sorts of tubes and equipment, this was no longer possible.
>
> I would have liked to stay with him in the evening and the night of his death, but the hospital asked us to go home. There was only limited room in intensive care and there were lots of patients. Early the next morning we were phoned and told that he had died. He travelled the last bit of his life without any of us there.
>
> At first, I was angry with myself that I had not followed my own feelings and stayed after all. I so much wanted to support him, particularly because I knew that he was afraid. But that is how it happened. It was a great consolation to us that the expression on his face was very peaceful and relaxed, with no traces of fear. Perhaps he was not alone after all...
>
> Fourteen days after his death a very curious thing happened. I had made an arrangement with a friend to spend the weekend with her. On Friday evening I suddenly felt unwell. I thought I was going to be ill and so I phoned to cancel the arrangement.
>
> I was sitting on the sofa and suddenly there was a very special atmosphere all around me. I had the feeling and

actually felt quite sure that my father was with me. This was not at all frightening. There was a voice in me which started to give all sorts of instructions. I did all sorts of things: I read poems, pieces from the Bible, from the Tibetan book of the Dead. I sang, talked, dredged up memories, made jokes – all talking out loud. This continued for the whole weekend. I felt very quiet inside; I was there, and yet I wasn't there. I hardly slept, but nevertheless I was very clear, and above all felt fulfilled.

I had the feeling that I was now able to do what I had not been able to do at the time of my father's death. I was unbelievably grateful for this. On Sunday afternoon I was finally able to say: 'Dad, you can go now, take the path you have to take. Its OK, we'll be together forever anyway.' At the moment I said this, the magic which had prevailed was broken, and I was alone again.[8]

This experience is important for our subject in several ways. We not only see that the dead person tries to make contact with his daughter, but also that the daughter intuitively feels how she can communicate with him at this level. In this way she fulfils the conditions which are necessary for contact between the living and the dead. To begin with, she relates to the person who has died as a living being. Then she remembers their shared memories which entail all sorts of feelings for both of them. In this way she makes a connection between their hearts. In fact, she also shares with her father in looking back and working on his life. It is not only the soul, but also the spirit which is given a special place in this dialogue. The dead father also needs some specific spiritual knowledge and insight which is available only on earth. Responding to this need, his daughter spontaneously reads poems to her dead father, as well as pieces from the Bible and the Tibetan Book of the Dead. By Sunday afternoon, it seems that he had received enough nourishment to be able to continue on his way in the spiritual world. The new connection had been made and will continue afterwards. The daughter told me that since that time, the contact with her father has continued and manifests itself in all sorts of ways.

The dead sometimes show themselves to their loved ones for a long time after their death, and may even enter into discussions with them.

A woman whose husband had died ten years previously felt that the contact with him had changed. It seemed to her as though he was much further away than she had experienced at first.

Once, when she was in her room on her own, she was overcome by a feeling of: 'Where are you?'. On the following night she met him. She told me: 'That night I had one of those dreams which is not a dream, but an encounter which you never forget. He appeared and showed me images from the past ten years of situations with me and the children. I asked him: "But do you know all this, then?" to which he lovingly answered: "But of course, I have been with you always."'9

Looking back at their life, the dead can also regret what they have done to others or what they have omitted to do. There are many stories about people who have died and who want to show their regret to those who have been left behind in all sorts of ways, and ask for their forgiveness. Sometimes these requests reach the living, though sometimes this happens indirectly, and sometimes they do not hear this request. Here are two examples.

A woman recounted how she had a very clear dream a few months after her father's death in which she met him. They walked arm-in-arm through a bright landscape with trees. As they walked together, the woman felt that she was 'on the other side'. Then her father started to talk to her. He told her that he had not been a very easy person and that he was aware of how he had let down his wife (the mother of the woman telling this story). Then he gave a message of love for his wife in a few clear sentences and asked the daughter to pass it on to her.

George Ritchie gave an example of an expression of regret which did not reach the person concerned: he was journeying through the astral world with the being of light and came across the following scene:

> In one house a younger man followed an older one from room to room. 'I'm sorry, Pa!' he kept saying. 'I didn't know what it would do to Mama! I didn't understand.'
>
> But though I could hear him clearly, it was obvious that the man he was speaking to could not. The old man was carrying a tray into a room where an elderly woman sat in bed. 'I'm sorry, Pa,' the young man said again. 'I'm sorry, Mama.' Endlessly, over and over, to ears that could not hear.

When Ritchie looked at the being of light, he felt his love and compassion following into the room. When he asked the being what the young man was so sorry about, the light next to him radiated the thought that the young man had killed himself and was now 'chained to the consequence of his act'.[10]

This is another example of someone who has died and who is imprisoned in the relationship with the loved ones he left behind. He is stuck and cannot find his way in the spiritual world because those who have remained behind cannot cope with their sorrow, and possibly their anger, and are therefore unable to forgive, or perhaps to realise that the dead soul seeks forgiveness. The dialogue that is needed on both sides has not taken place. It is only when this happens that it will be possible for both sides to

let go so that there is a liberation and the possibility of a new sort
of relationship between them.

To the extent that the dead are spiritually free, i.e. not entirely
taken up (any more) with looking back at their lives, they start to
fulfil tasks as a spiritual being which are reminiscent of the work
of (guardian) angels. There are numerous stories of people who
have been in a dangerous situation and whose lives were saved by
a dead person they had known. The following event took place
during the First World War.

> Will Bird was a Canadian fighting on the western front. At a
> certain point he was in a trench covered by a piece of
> tarpaulin. Suddenly the tarpaulin was pulled back and Will
> saw his brother Steve who had recently been killed. He
> indicated that Will should gather his belongings. A few
> minutes later a grenade exploded in exactly the place where
> Will had been sitting.[11]

But besides saving others from life-threatening situations, many
other inspirational influences are attributed to those who have
died. Artists, writers and musicians in particular have told how
they have been inspired by dead friends or members of the
family. Here are two examples.

Michel van der Plas who wrote many anthologies of poetry,
reflections and biographies, as well as cabaret songs, told how he
wrote an anthology of poems entitled 'Fatherland'.

Van der Plas: 'These poems were all about my father, his
country and his life. While I was writing them we were talking so
intensely together across the boundaries of death that his spirit
remained in my house for months.'[12]

In his memoirs, the musician and composer Hans-Georg
Burghardt wrote:

The pieces which I composed for the harmonium have an apparently unimportant, but actually very important place in my work. Carl Bergmann, who actually inspired this music, has been in the spiritual world for a long time. I am saying here that I could not have composed these special works for the harmonium and organ without his inspiration.[13]

Before Bergmann died in 1941, Burghardt and he had worked together for many years and been very close friends.

Both Van der Plas and Burghardt recognise that someone with whom they had been connected on earth continued to work intensely with them after death.

Harbingers of a new culture

It is possible that these sorts of experiences between the living and the dead are a harbinger of a future time when it will be quite normal for individuals on both sides of the threshold to consciously interact and communicate. In fact, we can assume that in the future there may again be a culture where it is commonplace for the living and the dead to support each other and offer to each other the insights each realm can give. A hint of this sort of future dialogue can be heard in the contacts which were established during the First World War between a young soldier in the German army who had died and his sisters who remained alive.

The soldier, Sigwart, was born in Munich in 1884. From his earliest years he showed great musical talent, and at the age of only eight he was composing songs which he accompanied himself, as well as pieces for the piano. Later he studied music and composed an opera. When the First World War broke out, he enlisted. On 9 May 1915 he was seriously injured by a shot through the lung. He died a few weeks later, aged 31.

Sigwart had a very special and close contact with some of his sisters. After his death he tried to reveal himself to them through some spiritual experiences. One of his sisters described these experiences as an inner restlessness which gave her a distinct feeling that Sigwart expected something from her. However, the idea of relating to Sigwart through spiritualism filled her with disgust and initially stopped her from exploring this further. But after a while she experienced an inner awakening and realised how she could contact Sigwart in a completely conscious way.[14]

She recounted:

> It became clear to me what Sigwart wanted. It is not that he wants to lead me by the hand and influence me from without; *I* have to open the door in my head and my heart *myself* so that I can hear the words which I must write down.

This was the beginning of a conversation between Sigwart and his sisters which was recorded and lasted for many years. In this ongoing conversation he described events in the spiritual world, gave his sisters advice about their spiritual life, helped them with meditations and prayers, and told them about his own experiences in the different spheres of the astral world and the higher world of light. He ascended to the higher worlds with part of his being relatively quickly, i.e., to the higher spheres of the astral world or world of the soul and the adjacent regions of the world of light, of devachan or the heavenly world. This was possible because he had already been deeply concerned with spiritual matters on earth.

We finish this chapter with a number of quotations from these discussions between Sigwart and his sisters. The reader will find many aspects confirmed which we discussed in previous chapters. To begin with, sorrow for the loss of their brother stood in the way of any contact between Sigwart and his sisters. Later, when they conquered their sorrow, the contact was better. At a certain point, Sigwart told them:

> I am very satisfied with you. At the beginning your pain was so dreadful for me. It was extremely difficult for me to make myself felt to you. It is better now.
>
> Because of your great love and insight I can come closer and closer to you. You will be happy because you will be able to go further through me and learn a great deal. I also died for you so that I would be able to pass you these spiritual insights.
>
> I evoked my death myself because I had something much greater to do here. You cannot imagine this work in any way: it is so great, so beautiful and so perfect.
>
> Although I go further all the while, I am always here and I always know how you are. We can find each other in all these higher matters – whether it is art, in prayers or in the beauty of nature, it does not make any difference. I can still feel every great thought. You must understand that from this sphere I can stay in contact with you because a high and pure love connects us and this will exist forever. You must believe this.
>
> Tonight I have already told you a great deal about my life and my death. You were all around me in a circle and we were happy to be together for a long time. Perhaps you will eventually remember this. First, I will appear to you in a dream.
>
> I am going to take a great deal of trouble to help you along, but to do this you must feel my presence as an encouragement to higher endeavours. I can only be with you when you are not influenced by outside energies, and you are entirely involved in an extrasensory atmosphere. As I no

longer have a body, this can only take place through the spiritual element. Therefore when you think of me, you must think of my spiritual self. Thinking about my physical body pulls me back into the material world all the time, and that is unpleasant.

When you talk about questions related to the spiritual world with spiritually advanced people, I can also benefit from this and learn a great deal from you which I do not experience here.

You want to know about my life here. I live only for the great work I have often told you about: the sacred music which will be extremely useful to mankind. What I created on earth was a tiny fragment of this. My creativity here will be something which will be extraordinarily beautiful and will penetrate all the spheres up to the very highest regions. However, you need a great deal of strength and talent for this. I have always had the feeling that I have had something tremendous to create. That is why I felt at peace when I went to war. I knew that everything was in God's hands. I did not regret it for a moment. That is how it had to be, it was my destiny. I always felt I would not grow old.

I have now arrived in a sphere where everything is easier. I am no longer so disturbed by the things which confused me at first. My work here is also much better, because it is freer of the influences of your earth. I have become more separate from it and therefore no longer share all the tiny concerns with you as I did at the beginning, which was very painful to me. Of course, every strong feeling related to me penetrates me immediately, but I am no longer burdened by all those hundreds of small cares and thoughts. I can mean much more for you now because I have greater strengths myself.

The bonds which connect us are much more intense than they were during my lifetime. Now I can be in you. I surround you with my help and love and I can protect you from the negative influences which life on earth still has. Call on me when you need me. My feeling of gratitude for you is constantly increasing because I can see how you develop for my sake. One day I will redeem this.

I am not only able to be with you, I can belong to you, absorb you, console you and strengthen you. But I cannot change anything in the course of your life.

Yesterday I was also present at your music and felt my strength in you. You must understand me. I am there and through my presence I unconsciously work with you. I am in the music you hear.

I left you because I have something great to do here. I have been commissioned to create seven heavenly symphonies. I have already completed one. The aim of these great creations is to guide feelings on earth along the right path. This music is spread through the different spheres which surround your world and has a tremendous influence. It spiritualises mankind. Music is the highest form of art. Only music can indirectly affect mankind. You cannot know or hear anything of this, because the earthly environment conceals it all and yet you listen to it. This is our work. People will hear it after their death.

The threads of our love become closer and closer and more and more beautiful. Invisible threads connect us, which is why we can respond to each other. Obviously this is easier for me because I no longer have a physical body and can immediately see any movement. For you, everything first has to pass through many dense layers. Therefore you do not feel every minor perception of expression from my side.

You are surrounded by restlessness today, which makes it difficult for me to talk to you. I can only do so when you have peace in you and around you. If there is no resounding echo because of a lack of harmony, my masters will only let me tell you half of what there is to say. Otherwise the sacred truths will be lost. 'The work' belongs to all of you, each of you individually, and will later also fulfil many other purposes.

Last night I heard your conversations. It is so wonderful when you are together and ask spiritual questions. I can answer you. Often you hear this, but unfortunately you often don't hear me. I can see how instructive this is for each of you because I can feel the effect on each of you individually. It is not only our own circle that is together. Many others also join us. They also exchange ideas and learn things and instruct both me and you. If you can keep on reading these spiritual texts and engaging in extrasensory questions at the same time on each occasion, I will be able to develop enormous strength in the future because higher beings always participate in this. They influence you and help you to solve the most difficult questions. I am always closest to you at that time and can also make myself felt as the strength I have becomes greater.

It is the hour of devotion. I bless you and I am in you. It helps us, it helps you and the divine being which guards you also helps. Hosts of beings of light come to this place of devotion. Have you never seen them? You can feel them so clearly. First you will feel them, later you will see them.

I have heard you sing the dear old tunes. Every note means

something to me, it is a whisper of the time when we were still together. There is a melancholy there which is deeper than memory. Come often and bring me some higher thoughts. It is your task to build the most beautiful temple. Every higher thought is a building block and an infinite number are needed. Give me the building blocks.

The further you go spiritually, the greater is the circle of beings to whom you give your love. After all, you do not love just one person on earth. This is what is so wonderful: the great harmony works like a beautifully tuned chord. Every note can be heard, but perfection lies in the harmony of all the notes together.

The greatest moment was today, when my brother went to my last resting place. He was strong. I was able to come close to him. My higher self embraced him in a cloud of love and peace. From now on there will not be a moment where I will be afraid. Nothing can separate us anymore. This was the last test for me. You have survived this and therefore I have been liberated! I close my eyes in humility for the fulfilment of my desires which were also yours. Look for me only in the lightest heights, in the wide halls of peace.

Notes

1   *Trouw*, 10 March 1997.
2   Martin Burckhard: *Die Erlebnisse nach dem Tod*
3   Rudolf Steiner: *Okkulte Untersuchungen über das Leben zwischen Tod und neuer Geburt*
4   Ibid
5   F. Rittelmeyer, *Meine Lebensbegegnungen mit Rudolf Steiner*, chapter 9
6   Matthew 18:20.
7   Kenneth Ring/Evelyn Elsaesser Valarino: *Lesson From the Light: What We Can Learn from the Near-Death Experience*

8   Letter from N.N.
9   R. Zeylmans: *Stervensbegeleiding*
10 George Ritchie: *Return from Tomorrow*
11 Richard Heijster in *Trouw*, 5 December 1998
12 *Trouw*, 30 November 1998
13 *Motief*, February 1999
14 *The Bridge over the River.* The quotes which follow all come from this book.

13. What Can We Do for the Dead?

Here on earth, we can do and mean much more for those who have died than we often think.

* Sometimes we can provide very concrete help to those who are imprisoned in the astral world.
* Through prayers, we can awaken those who have become lost in the dark of the astral world and make them conscious of the light which lives in them and is waiting for them.
* We can help those who reside in the spiritual world in purgatory or kamaloka to acquire awareness and insight to harvest the fruits of the lives they have just completed.
* We can inspire the dead on their way through the spiritual world by offering them the gift of our gratitude, trust and openness for the future. This seemingly 'simple' gift has enormous spiritual strength and therefore has a great effect on the dead to whom we offer it with love.

Help for those who are imprisoned in the astral world

I have experienced myself in a very impressive way how we can actually help the dead here on earth and support them on their path through the spiritual world.

When my sister died a few years ago, I was sitting on the sofa at home a few days after her death. I lit a candle for her, said a prayer silently and was with her in my thoughts. Suddenly and quite unexpectedly I found myself outside my body in a world of spirits. I saw all sorts of people walking to and fro as transparent spirits. I noticed that although there were many figures walking around, they did not see each other. Sometimes they walked straight through one another without noticing. They were constantly moving, as though they were unable to rest. I felt that I had a task to carry out here, though I did not know what task this could be. Suddenly I saw my sister sitting on a rock. She was crying and I heard her say: 'What should I do now?' As soon as I saw her, I knew that I had to go there for her. I went straight up to her and urged her to go towards the light. Then it happened: I saw how she suddenly shot up, and clad in an elliptical, transparent cloak, flew higher and higher into space. I heard a swishing sound like that of a rocket which increased as she moved faster. I watched her, happy and surprised: she became smaller and smaller until there was only a dot in the distance.

The next moment I was back in my body, opened my eyes, and I was sitting on the sofa back at home. For days I silently carried within me the emotion and joy which this experience had given me. When I reflected on this experience, what really struck me was how appropriate it was in the whole pattern of things. My sister did not like strange, unexpected situations; she was happiest with familiar things. But now she was confronted with a new world which she had to enter alone and where she had to find her way with her own strength. During her life on earth she would always have had a member of the family with her in this sort of situation. But when she passed into the spiritual world this was not possible. That is why I had been allowed to give her the one little push she needed to find her way in the new world.

Ever since, I have been full of a deep sense of gratitude that I was able to do this.

Later I again saw how someone else I was closely related to during her life on earth and who had been 'stuck' in the astral world since her death, finally found her way to the light; I saw her too shoot upwards towards the world of light from the dark, like a rocket. The fact that she had been 'stuck' in the dark for so many years by earthly standards, was not only a result of her inability to let go of the earth, and of life on earth, but also because of her strong focus on herself which made it difficult for her to see others, and because of her lack of trust in God. I saw how our prayers, my own and those of others, eventually helped her to awaken from this anaesthetised state and acquire an inner awareness of dawning light. This consciousness enabled her to find her way to the world of light and arrive there in the end.

Many people have experienced such things consciously in our time. There are also people who have unconsciously – for instance during their sleep – entered these areas of the spiritual world, waking people there and helping them to move on.

Everyone who has these experiences and assimilates them as a conscious memory becomes aware of the fact that here on earth we can certainly have an influence on the path of those who have died and who have started on their journey through the spiritual world. It shows that they do not become inaccessible to us, but can be reached and that we can influence the other person's journey in that world.

One of the first things which becomes clear when we reflect on the question of what we can do here on earth for those who have passed on is: I can pray for them. Every prayer which comes from our heart is a spiritual force which will really reach them and in some way have an effect. In particular, we can pray for those who are in some way 'stuck' in the astral world, unable to find their way to the light. If we pray regularly, this also means that a force of light goes to them from the earth which will awaken them step by step, making them more conscious and aware in their spiritual surroundings.

You could also say that this repeated prayer is a task which the spiritual world has entrusted to us. We can learn to work together with the spiritual beings, the angels, and help free those who are imprisoned.

Helping those who reside in the astral world

But we can do even more. Our influence, or the effect of the forces of our heart, not only has an impact on those who are stuck in the astral world, but can reach beyond this. This influence becomes quite understandable when we think about the experiences those who have died undergo in kamaloka or the astral world.

In fact the same process of reflection also takes place in *us* when a loved one or someone we were closely related to dies. We are not only confronted with feelings of loss, with questions which arise and for which we do not immediately have an answer, and extremely painful feelings of sorrow, but often also with feelings of anger and abandonment.

All these questions and feelings mean that we automatically start to reflect about who the other person really was, and his place in our life. We start to think about what the other person gave us and what we would not have learned or discovered without him, as well as how the other person made life difficult for us, often unintentionally. In this process of reflection we can become aware of things which we did not see or were unable to see during the person's life. We start to see both ourselves and the other person in a more honest and clearer way.

Of course, we can also avoid this process of reflection. We can avoid or suppress the questions which arise. This is possible, but fortunately it does not happen in most cases. When, however, we pursue this process of reflection, become inwardly active and allow the process to take place, we not only grow towards greater insight and clarity ourselves but also give the person who has died some insight and understanding. It is as though the one who has died looks with us over our shoulder and can read in our heart what is growing there as insight and understanding. What those who have died read in this way can greatly stimulate and facilitate the process they are going through themselves.

When the dead become aware, in the astral world, of certain mistakes they have made, it may help them if they can read in our hearts that we have also become aware of these mistakes, but that at the same time we have understood *why* such mistakes were made. It may be helpful to the dead to read in our hearts that we have truly forgiven them, because it was not the mistakes that were important, but the good things they gave us. Usually we do not notice it consciously, but the insights which the dead acquire in the astral world can also enter our own hearts and knowledge, at least if we are open to such things and do not go out of our way to avoid painful questions.

Therefore we see that this mutual reflection which takes place both in the astral world and here on earth can be an inspiring force that not only helps but also unites the living and the dead. It is possible for the love which existed between two such people – one here on earth, the other in the spiritual world – to shine out, purified of all that hampered it before.

For those of us who remain here on earth, it is important to know that we can help the other person by not avoiding the questions which arise in us, but by confronting these questions as openly and honestly as possible. By doing so we not only create a new path to the future for ourselves, but also for the other person.

It is only when we are at peace with the past and are able to let go of it, once it has been processed and assimilated, that the future truly opens up to us. We are no longer chained to the past, but stand in the present, free and ready to move on.

I would like to emphasise that when someone has passed on to the other side, he can both *receive* forgiveness from other people and *grant* forgiveness to them. It is not too late to achieve reconciliation, which did not come about on earth for one reason or another. It is also possible to reveal this reconciliation to each other. Someone who has died can reveal this to us from the spiritual world, for example in a dream, in meditation or as a sudden feeling of enlightenment, an inner certainty. For our part, we can reveal this reconciliation to the person who has died by expressing it in a prayer, in a letter that we read out loud or simply in the stillness of our own heart. This reconciliation is always the result of inner reflection and confrontation we have *both* engaged in after someone has died. It does not have to wait for a subsequent life on earth. It is very moving to become aware of these possibilities and to experience how such reconciliation can become a profound reality.

Inspiring loved ones on their journey through the spiritual world

Great gifts we can and should offer from the earth to those who have died include gratitude, trust and a new focus for the future. These three gifts can profoundly determine the path of the individual passing through the spiritual world after death. We will therefore consider their effects one by one.

Gratitude

The gift of gratitude is the first one. For the final question which emerges at the end of a process of reflection when a loved one has died is this: Can I be truly grateful for the role which that person played in my life? Can I be grateful for everything he gave to me as experience? This also includes being grateful for all sorts of difficult or painful experiences.

It is not difficult to be grateful for beautiful and great experiences: this gratitude seems to well up automatically in our hearts. But painful experiences are another matter. It is easy to react with a sense of bitterness or vengeance. And yet we can come to see that in some way, perhaps not yet fully clear to us, we needed these difficult and painful experiences because we would not otherwise have become the people we are now.

If we can transcend all sense of bitterness and vengeance, seeing what we were able to learn through such painful experiences, we can develop a sense of gratitude. If this gratitude grows in us step by step, it becomes a spiritual force which flows straight from our own heart to the other person, and serves as a tremendous stimulus in his process of reflection in the astral world. It will help the one who has died to move through feelings of disappointment or bitterness and in the end develop gratitude too.

With gratitude comes a sense of peace at what was completed during life on earth, enabling us to let go of that life more easily and move on. Even when the other person has moved on into the world of light from the astral world, our gratitude will still continue to be a tremendous inspiration on the journey through spiritual spheres. To put it in simple terms, our gratitude gives wings to the one who has died. It is by no means an unimportant force that we set in motion with our gratitude.

But we should realise that such gratitude does not only relate to what the one who has died gave us during his life on earth. Personal gratitude can be incorporated in a total sense of gratitude: can I be grateful to *God* for everything which I experience in this life and everything that happens to me? Can I be grateful to God for absolutely every aspect of my life's destiny, the dark and the light, the happy and the sad, the lonely and the joyful experiences?

This is not an easily won insight, or a question we can answer immediately. The answer can only mature after years of struggling with ourselves and with the pain and disappointments of life. However, if we can eventually arrive at unconditional and total gratitude this becomes a spiritual force that reaches and inspires all our loved ones on the other side, and through them the whole spiritual world. The effects of this are very far-reaching and cannot be overestimated.

This is a very strange notion for many people, since gratitude is not a feeling that usually plays much part in relationships on earth. However, in the spiritual world gratitude is the very fabric underlying everything. It is the very basis of that world!

Gratitude is not something you can acquire by reading a few pages, but something which takes a whole lifetime. A lifetime of inner conflict with all those dark feelings of the lower ego which stand in the way: fear, a feeling of being hard done-by, misunderstanding, uncertainty and so on. Every step forwards on this path is also a gift for the spiritual world, and brings us a response from that world as well.

Trust

What we have said here in general terms about gratitude also applies to the next gift which we can pass on to those who have died: our trust.

In the first place, this means having trust that the person will be received into the spiritual world and be supported and accompanied there. When we have to let go of someone who is dying, there are other hands which take over this care and support from us. None pass through the gate of death entirely on their own. Everyone receives help. It is important that our inner eyes are open for this reality. We can surround and envelop those who are dying with this trust, and this helps them on their way too.

In addition, we can also trust in the spiritual force and light active in the dying person. After all, every person carries divine light within him. At some point this light will manifest itself. This awareness can also help us to let go of the one who is dying with peace in our heart.

If we are able to feel inner trust, this becomes a spiritual force which starts to radiate in our heart and directly reaches out to embrace and inspire the dying person with a sense of well-being. This trust, as a spiritual force, is so strong that it can give the dying person wings.

In addition to our trust in the dying person and in the spiritual beings receiving him, the trust we have in life is also important. This may be even more difficult. We often feel that we are so alone, so lost and so torn when we have to let go of loved ones and let them go their own way freely in the spiritual world. We feel as though we are amputated, as though something in ourselves has died. Yet still we have to trust that we are not alone in this sadness and loneliness, that something sustains and helps us, that a new path will open up – although it seems as if a path has just been closed. Life has a deeper meaning and significance. The awareness of that gives us the strength to continue – on our own.

It is this trust that saves us from becoming entrenched in bitterness and disappointment for the rest of our days, and allows us to feel that God is with us, even in the midst of our sorrow. And it is this trust that makes it possible to experience God's closeness in a very private, personal and intimate way.

It is no small matter to learn to feel this trust, particularly during a very dark period in our life. But if we can manage it, this also gives us one of the greatest spiritual treasures which life on earth can offer. We acquire something that cannot be undermined by anything or anyone, because it has already been tried and tested by the dark forces of loss and death. Anyone who has put down roots in this trust and acquired the spiritual strength to be resolute and open through great hardship, radiates strength back into the spiritual world to illuminate and inspire the life there. Therefore our growth in trust is a gift which not only has an effect on people living on earth with us, but also on those living in the spiritual world.

One of the moving things about reflecting on these gifts we can pass on to our loved ones in the spiritual world is that they are entirely gifts from ourselves: we first have to acquire them and turn them into inner reality before we can pass them on to our loved ones as a gift, for only then do they have the strength to ascend to spiritual worlds.

Openness to the future

The third gift which we can pass on to our loved ones beyond the threshold of death is inner openness to the future. This means developing a sense of unprejudiced curiosity, and allowing the future to come towards us. This is by no means easy. The loss of a loved one often chains us to memories and to the past, preventing us from looking towards the future without any preconceived ideas. Sorrow and loss are such strong emotional forces in us that all our attention is focused on what was, on what we have lost and how things could have been if the other person had not died. So after the loss of a loved one we often live more in the past than in the present, and do not focus on the future at all. It is only after a long time of coming to terms with this loss, and learning to accept it in our lives, that it is possible to create space for the future again, step by step.

This third gift, an untrammelled openness to the future, is

therefore also one which we first have to create in ourselves before we can send it to our loved ones who have died as a spiritual force.

People often remain stuck in bitterness and sadness after losing a loved one, precisely because they are afraid to plumb the depths of sorrow and loss in order to be able to let go. However, if we allow our bitterness and paralysed grief to deflect us, these can turn into forces which actually get in the way of our loved ones finding their own way in the spiritual world. It is as though we constantly pull them back into the past, back into life on earth, instead of sending them the encouragement and incentives to continue on their own path. What we do with our own grief and how we miss them, the way in which we deal with this, certainly has its effect on their onward journey – either positively or negatively.

It is sometimes wrongly thought that we should not be sad at all, or that we should not wish that the other person were still here in our own life, close to us. But such feelings are quite natural and normal, and an intrinsic and essential part of the mourning process. The important thing is whether we hold onto these feelings, without working through them. We should try to have the courage to go through pain and loss with all the sorrow that it entails, for otherwise we may shut out such feelings and fail to resolve them. We could then become cold and bitter. Everyone has a choice in this, and makes a choice, whether or not they are conscious of it. This choice has a direct effect on the journey of the loved one in the spiritual world.

If we have the courage to go through this mourning process fully, we may find at a certain point that all our inner experiences have made us a different person: we start to think and see things differently. We become more sensitive to the pain and sadness of others, more conscious of life's meaning, aware of the silent guidance and help of God. We may feel something like: I would never have chosen this, and I would not like to experience such a period of loss and sadness again, but I feel that in the end I have achieved some inner maturity as a result of it. Finally we are open to the future again and released from the shackles of the past which prevented us from living in the 'here and now'. We have acquired an inner strength which we can now pass on to the one who had died as a gift.

This third gift is possibly the best and most valuable one we can give to the other person, for it requires all our spiritual strength and all our belief to achieve and create it ourselves first. It is however more than worth the effort, for it opens up a new future, not only for ourselves, but also for the other person in the spiritual world and our relationship with each other. This gift gives the one who has died a new horizon and a view beyond our imagination into the new world which he has entered.

Before going to sleep at night

We are closer to the spiritual world at night than during the daytime. During the day, our attention is (justifiably) focused on all sorts of things which have to happen on earth or which are matters of concern and require our attention. But at night we can cast off these cares, becoming more open to what comes to us from the spiritual world.

This is why the night is the best time to enter into contact with our loved ones who have crossed the threshold of death. This often takes place unconsciously, but we can also try to bring some awareness to bear on it. For example, you may be in bed, have read a little, then turn the light off and want to go to sleep. If you think of the person who has died at that moment, just before you fall asleep, this becomes a strength which passes directly to the one in the spiritual world.

The question is therefore: what do you want to pass to the

person who has died? Of course it is best if we do not pass our feelings of loss and sadness to him, so much as our feelings of gratitude and trust. But how do you do this? You can do it by recalling memories of the other person, preferably some of the best and happiest memories that you have. Think of this memory while you lie quietly in bed, and allow the memory to pass through you in such a way that it becomes reality for a moment, so that you start to radiate warmth. If you do this, it is likely that you will feel a warm happiness and grateful feeling within you. Allow this warmth to pass right through you. With your eyes closed, look at this memory and feel it fully. Then let it go, and go to sleep. At that moment you have sent a message of love and gratitude, and the other person will have received and felt the contact of the loving warmth which came from you. You can be sure that the message arrived. Feelings of true love always reach the other person wherever he or she may be, on earth or in heaven.

There is a chance that during the night you will dream about the loved one who has died – a dream which is more than a dream, because it actually is a real encounter in the spiritual world. This encounter is made possible by the gift of warmth and gratitude which you sent towards the other person from your heart, before you went to sleep.

Love is eternal and even death cannot put an end to love. This is why it is possible to continue to reach and help our loved ones, even when they have entered the wider, further realms of the spiritual world.

Bibliography

Anon: *The Bridge over the River*, Anthroposophic Press, New York 1995

Burckhardt, Martin: *Die Erlebnisse nach dem Tod*, Die Pforte, Dornach 1996

Eijk, P van der: *Naar het hiernamaals en terug*, BZZToH, Gravenhage 1991

Drake, S.: *Though You Die*, Floris Books 2002

Flynn, Charles P.: *After the Beyond: Human Transformation and the Near-Death Experience*, Prentice Hall Inc., Englewood Cliffs, New Jersey, 1986.

Klijn, A.F.J.: *Apocriefen van het Nieuwe Testament I*, Kampen 1981

Linden, Carel ter: *Een land waar je de weg niet kent*, Meinema 1995

Moody, Raymond: *Life After Life*, BCA 2001

Moody, Raymond: *Life After Loss*, Rider 2001

Moody, Raymond: *The Light Beyond*, Bantam Books New York, l988.

Ring, Kenneth; Valarino, Evelyn Elsaesser: *Lessons from the Light: What we can Learn from the Near-Death Experience*. Insight Books/Plenum Publishing Corp. New York/London, l998.

Ritchie, George: *Return from Tomorrow*, Baker Book House 1978

Rittelmeyer, F.: *Gemeinschaft mit den Verstorbenen*, Verlag Urachhaus, Stuttgart, 1978

Rittelmeyer, F.: *Das Heilige Jahr*, Verlag Urachhaus, Stuttgart, 1959

Rittelmeyer, F.: *Meine Lebensbegegnung mit Rudolf Steiner*, Verlag Urachhaus, Stuttgart, 1928

Steiner, Rudolf: *Esoteric Christianity*, Rudolf Steiner Press, London 2000

Steiner, Rudolf: *Life Beyond Death*, Rudolf Steiner Press, London 1995

Steiner, Rudolf: *Evil*, Rudolf Steiner Press, London 1997

Steiner, Rudolf: *Theosophy*, Rudolf Steiner Press, London 1970

Steiner, Rudolf: *Aus den Inhalten der esoterischen Stunden III*, lecture 6th January 1913, GA 266/111, Verlag der Rudolf Steiner-Nachlassverwaltung, Dornach, 1998

Steiner, Rudolf: *The Gospel of St John*, Rudolf Steiner Press, London 1988

Steiner, Rudolf: *Okkulte Untersuchungen über das Leben zwischen Tod und neuer Geburt*, GA 140, lecture 2, 20th February 1913, Verlag der Rudolf Steiner-Nachlassverwaltung, Dornach, 1970

Ruijsbeek,E van, Messing M: *Het evangelie van Thomas*, Ankh-Hermes, Deventer,

The Gospel according to Nicodemus, Anthroposophical Foundation, 1981

143

About the Authors

Margarete van den Brink works as an organisation and communication consultant – also in the UK – and writes books. One previous book by her was published in English: *More Precious than Light* (Hawthorn Press, 1995).

Hans Stolp studied theology and worked for many years as a radio pastor. He is well known in the Netherlands for his books and courses on esoteric Christianity.

More Precious than Light
How dialogue can transform relationships and build Community
Margarete van den Brink

Profound changes are taking place as people awaken to the experience of the Christ in themselves, and in significant human encounter. As tradition fades, individual and social paths of growth emerge. These are helped by building relationships through helping conversations, through dialogue, through exploring heartfelt questions which can lead to liberating personal insights.

'The true community spirit values differences as well as harmony, is open rather than closed. Challenge, support, questioning and empathy are all needed. Knowing when one or the other is appropriate depends on presence of mind. It depends as much on intuition as on a knowledge of group work.'

160pp; 216 x 138mm; 1 869 890 83 3; paperback

Getting in touch with Hawthorn Press

We would be delighted to hear your feedback on our books, how they can be improved, and what your needs are. Visit our website for details of forthcoming books and events at **www.hawthornpress.com**

Ordering books

If you have difficulties ordering Hawthorn Press books from a bookshop, you can order online at **www.hawthornpress.com** or you can order direct from:

United Kingdom
Booksource
32 Finlas Street, Glasgow
G22 5DU
Tel: (08702) 402182
Fax: (0141) 557 0189
E-mail: orders@booksource.net

USA/North America
SteinerBooks
PO Box 960, Herndon
VA 20172-0960
Tel: (800) 856 8664
Fax: (703) 661 1501
E-mail: service@steinerbooks.org

Dear Reader

If you would like a catalogue please fill in your name and address and return to Hawthorn Press:

Name
_____

Address
_____

_____

_____

_____

Postcode
_____

Tel. no.
_____

Please return to: Hawthorn Press, Hawthorn House,
1 Lansdown Lane, Stroud, Glos. GL5 1BJ, UK
or Fax (01453) 751138